Spiritual Therapy

Combining Psychotherapy with the Gospel For A Better You!

by

M. Jim Shelton L.C.S.W.

ISBN 1-930679-99-8

Archive Publishers

754 East 50 North
Heber City, UT 84032

435-654-0824
www.archivepublishers.com

2004

More comments from readers . . .

Jim Shelton's book *Spiritual Therapy* has been of great value to me both personally and professionally. As a practicing attorney, I have been able to use the principles taught in the book to help my clients make better decisions and to seek professional help as needed. As a Latter-day Saint, the experiences Jim shares in his book have helped me realize more fully the love of our Savior, Jesus Christ, and how much He wants to help me return to His presence. Jim is a wise and kind friend who has shared the knowledge he has gained over many years to bless the lives of all who will take the time to read this wonderful book.

Frank Mohlman
Attorney

Jim Shelton's book *Spiritual Therapy* has given me many important tools to help me find strengths in myself that I didn't know I had. After being his client for over a year and reading his book, I not only hope for a happier and more peaceful life through the atonement of Jesus Christ, but I now work for one by changing the core beliefs about myself to positive ones. I've recommended his book to my friends and family in the hope that it will touch their lives as it has mine.

Susana Campbell
Homemaker and mother of 8

Jim Shelton has written a very nice, user-friendly book in *Spiritual Therapy*. Professionals and consumers alike will find it to be a concise summary of the parallels between cognitive therapy and spiritual concepts. He is able to clearly explain principles that most people can implement fairly easily. Readers will find the book to be useful and practical. *Spiritual Therapy* could be recommended as support reading to anyone with a spiritual background who is currently engaged in the process of cognitive therapy (counseling).

Matt Watson, LCSW
Supervisor
LDS Family Services

Like many people, I grew up in a dysfunctional family. Ours had an alcoholic father. My response to that environment was an attraction to addictive personalities with me in the role of enabler. For years I sought to change this behavior through faith without combining it with clinical practice. This faith-alone approach was sometimes helpful, but familiar behavior patterns continued to occur. When I read *Spiritual Therapy*, a light, a ray of hope entered my life. I could feel that combining professional ideas with spiritual concepts bridges the void between the two. Also, I found the book very readable and enjoyable. I refer to it often for guidance in my quest to heal. I value this book so much that I introduced it to my bishop and stake presidency with the hope that they will use it to assist in people-problems they encounter. *Spiritual Therapy* is a book that can change lives.

Bonita Robertson, MS, RN
Head of Nursing (retired)
Salt Lake Comm. College

Jim Shelton offers amazingly simple and effective solutions to complex dilemmas and problems that everyone faces. The pages of *Spiritual Therapy* shine with his warmth, humility, wisdom and experience. This book is mandatory reading for anyone seeking to build, heal, and improve his life!

Cliff R. Passey, M.Ed., MSW
LDS Seminary Teacher

If hope is a vision of God's promises and the road that leads to them, then Jim Shelton has written a very hopeful book. He himself has walked the road leading out of depression, and that in itself is a message of hope. The cognitive therapy he espouses can silence the internal voices that tear at our hope of healing and wholeness, allowing the Savior's voice to speak peace and promise. I recommend this book, *Spiritual Therapy*, to anyone seeking these blessings.

Larry Lewis, L.P.C.
Clinical Supervisor
LDS Family Services

Over the years that I have worked as a therapist, I have thought many times how I conceive my work in a spiritual paradigm. Jim Shelton has masterfully written the book that I wish I had written, as he captured the essence of spiritual therapy in his treatise *Spiritual Therapy*. Using the scriptures, principles of righteousness, the best of social work practice and many clinical illustrations, Jim distilled the core truths of a spiritual paradigm which has as its change agent the Savior. As I read and reread *Spiritual Therapy*, it has affirmed what I believe about the repentance process that true healing, or acceptance of things which cannot change, is always a spiritual gift predicated upon our own strivings and the Lord's mercy to us as his children.

Betsy Chatwin, L.C.S.W.
Therapist, LDS Family Services
Author, *Reaching for Hope*

About the author . . .

Mark Jim Shelton was born and raised in the Idaho Falls area. He attended BYU and graduated with high honors and a bachelors degree in psychology in 1979. He completed a successful mission to Germany. He graduated with a masters degree in social work from the University of Utah in 1982 and has worked as a mental health therapist for the last twenty years. He currently works for Valley Mental Health in Tooele, Utah, and LDS Family Services. He has served in several church callings including gospel doctrine instructor; counselor in a bishopric; high councilor; and bishop. He currently serves in a calling which brings particular enjoyment – the primary chorister. Jim Shelton is married to Jerilyn Zenk Shelton and together they are the parents of five children.

CONTENTS

In the Beginning   1

1. Change   7

2. Cognitive Therapy   13

3. Atonement   23

4. Tying It Together   27

5. Perfectionism   35

6. Excessive Responsibility   43

7. Neglecting Our Own Needs   53

8. Sagging Self Image   63

9. Anxiety   73

10. Anger   85

11. Addictions   93

12. Other Factors   110

13. Day by Day   120

14. Trials   131

15. Conclusion   138

References   143

Introduction
In the beginning . . .

When I started my graduate studies in 1979, religion and things remotely resembling religion were taboo topics. They were just not spoken of. Even at the University of Utah, where I completed my graduate studies, there were several faculty members who were LDS, and still religion was not mentioned at all. As I furthered my graduate studies, any references at all to religion were generally negative.

Many clinicians and therapists have considered religion damaging to their patients. Psychotherapists as prominent as Sigmund Freud considered religion as a form of pathology. Albert Ellis, one of the founders of cognitive therapy, was downright antagonistic to religion. He is quoted as saying in 1988, "devout, orthodox, or dogmatic religion is significantly correlated with emotional disturbances, because devoutly religious people tend to be inflexible, closed, intolerant and unchanging. The elegant therapeutic solution to emotional problems is to be quite unreligious" (1) Statements like these discouraged me but I pressed on in my graduate studies and I pressed on in my goal to be an active, devout LDS therapist.

Fortunately, statements such as those made by Dr. Ellis about religion have proven to be quite wrong. Multiple studies in recent years have shown quite the opposite. Regular church attendance and other religious practices such as prayer have shown to be very beneficial to our physical health. One does not have to go far to find research bearing this out. Such elite universities as Princeton, Duke, Harvard and George

Spiritual Therapy

Washington University have produced research findings that support the beneficial effect of regular religious worship on our health. Regular church attendance is positively correlated with lowered blood pressure, lower rates of certain types of cancer, coronary artery disease, cirrhosis of the liver and other diseases. (2)

Even in my field of mental health, the results are encouraging. In a 1990 study of 451 African-American men and women, those who were religiously involved had significantly lower rates of depression. The non-religious men in this particular study were twice as likely to suffer from depression than their religious counterparts. (3) In another study in 1992 of 1,110 male patients at the Veterans Administration hospital, those who reported that religion helped them to cope were much less likely to suffer from depression than those who did not report using religion as a means of coping. (4)

I am so thankful to certain courageous individuals in my field who went against the tide and who spoke in favor of incorporating religion into clinical practice. Allen Bergin, a psychologist at Brigham Young University, is one such individual. He has argued convincingly that people who are religious or spiritual are generally more mentally healthy. Dr. Bergin has been involved in a series of public debates with Albert Ellis on the topic of religion, and he has more than held his own in these debates and has argued impressively in favor of religion. Dr. Bergin has since retired but the torch has been passed to other psychologists at BYU. Albert Ellis has shown signs of softening. In a conference I attended at the Veterans Hospital in Salt Lake City in April, 1998, Dr. Albert Ellis listed eight points of agreement between Christianity and his form of cognitive therapy, Rational Emotive Behavioral therapy. He seemed to be admitting that therapy and religion can peacefully co-exist and that they share many of the same goals and principles. I am including these eight points at the end of this Introduction.

Other well-known psychologists and psychiatrists have made combining religion and spirituality with clinical practice more acceptable in recent years. Dr. Scott Peck, a renowned psychiatrist, wrote a best-selling book, The Road Less Traveled, that is on the bookshelf of almost every clinician in the U. S. In this book, he speaks ardently in favor of religion and spirituality being integrally involved in the therapeutic process. Now that it is popular, religious therapists are coming out of the woodwork. Spirituality and religious worship is unashamedly being incorporated into their therapeutic framework. In every mental health conference that I have attended in recent years, there has been at least one workshop about how to incorporate religion and spirituality into clinical practice. Carl Jung, the famous German psychoanalyst and disciple of Freud, has been re-discovered by therapists. Jung wrote extensively about religion in his books and essays and went so far as saying that he could only heal those who embraced religion and spirituality in their lives. (5) It's as if Cinderella (religion) had suddenly married the prince and there is a new-found respect for her. The step-mother (psychiatry) and her two step-daughters (psychology and social work) are very much vying to gain favor with the public by aligning themselves with religion.

In the LDS Church, most members and leaders seem to recognize that therapy can be beneficial. However, I have discovered there is also a degree of mistrust and suspicion among many members and leaders, especially among many men, towards therapy. A small minority of bishops and Church leaders view therapy as foolishness and a complete waste. Some may even go so far as to view therapy and counseling as contrary to the gospel. I hope to be able to show in this book that the gospel and therapy are not only compatible but that they ultimately come from the same mold. The healing that comes from the gospel and the healing that comes from therapy come from the same source i.e. the Holy Ghost. Of course, not all therapies are created equal. Certain types of therapy may very well be harmful but I will clearly explain in this book how to differentiate between good and bad therapy. I practice cognitive therapy and, in spite of what Albert Ellis said years ago, it is very compatible with the gospel of Jesus Christ. I will demonstrate this in the following chapters. There is no reason to fear or mistrust therapy and, in fact, we should openly embrace both therapy and the gospel.

Common Values Between Christianity and Rational
Emotive Behavioral Therapy
By Albert Ellis Ph.D. (April, 1998)

1. Christianity and R.E.B.T. both agree on free will to a certain extent

2. R.E.B.T. advocates self-acceptance and people are essentially good. Christianity accepts the sinner but not the sin.

3. R.E.B.T. advocates high frustration tolerance and Christianity also advocates high frustration tolerance.

4. R.E.B.T. advocates accepting others. Christianity says love your neighbor.

5. R.E.B.T. believes achievement is not essential to happiness. Christians also believe the meek shall inherit the earth.

6. R.E.B.T teaches that love and attachment are good but love is not a need but highly desirable. Christians also teach God's approval is essential but others' approval is not necessary for happiness.

7. R.E.B.T. encourages responsibility for feelings and behaviors and Christians also teach people to be responsible.

8. R.E.B.T. and Christianity both agree man is not perfect. Only God is perfect.

CHAPTER 1

Change

I love to see people change. It has been a marvelous and wonderful experience to assist people in the change process in several capacities as a missionary, bishop and therapist. When I witness change, I feel honored and often feel like Moses on Mount Sinai that I am standing on holy ground. One of the most joyous experiences in life is to help our family, friends and those we care about change their lives. Those of you who have been on missions have undoubtedly experienced this great joy. So many missionaries at the end of their missions say that their missions were the best two years of their lives. The reason for this is because they have been instruments of change and in this process of changing others they have also been uplifted and elevated. It leads to an over flowing of happiness and prompts great missionaries, such as Ammon in the *Book of Mormon*, to exclaim: "My joy is full, yea, my heart is brim with joy, and I will rejoice in my God." (Alma 26:11).

Of course, missionaries do not have a monopoly on this joy. Many bishops, Relief Society presidents, Young Men and Young Women leaders, home teachers and visiting teachers and others have experienced the same outpouring of happiness when they have successfully helped someone change. I have been blessed to be in such roles in the Church. The memories I have as a missionary and a bishop of people converted and lives changed stand out like diamonds in my mind. I will always treasure those times. I have also been blessed to be in the change business as a therapist. The change that I witness as a therapist is just as rewarding and fulfilling as the happiness I have experienced as a missionary and a bishop. This has led me to wonder how change occurs. It has led me to ask, as Enos did: "Lord, how is it done?" (Enos v.7) Is the change that occurs through the gospel the same change that occurs through psychotherapy? It is the main premise of this book to answer this question affirmatively. This is not something commonly taught in graduate school. Many professionals do not recognize the connection between spiritual conversion and the change that occurs in therapy. However, after being involved in therapy for twenty years I can testify that the same uplifting feelings I had as a bishop or a missionary are the same kind of emotions I feel on a frequent basis in my profession. I have no doubt these joyous feelings originate with the Holy Ghost. This is the main reason I love my job so much. It is an honor and great pleasure to be part of the change that occurs in my clients' lives. Although the vehicle of change may be different, the change that occurs through therapy is the same change that occurs through religious conversion. It all comes about through the power and miracle of the atonement of Jesus Christ.

There are many good examples of change in the scriptures. Enos is such an example. When one reads about Enos in the *Book of Mormon*, one gets the impression he was not a spiritual giant before his repentance and conversion. He was probably much like any other youth with the same foibles and weaknesses that youth commonly possess. He did have a strong desire, however, to experience the same joy that his father had experienced through Jesus Christ. His soul "hungered" and he did "wrestle" all day long to know God and receive a remission of his sins. He did finally receive a remission of his sins and his "guilt was swept away". He was made "whole:" through the atonement of Christ. Enos was never the same after this experience. He truly changed and dedicated his life to preaching and testifying the gospel. The change that occurred to Enos as a young man stayed with him until the end of his life.

Therapy can be effectively combined with the gospel to achieve many of the same goals of peace of conscience. life long change, and becoming whole. Some are suspicious of the change that occurs through therapy. Some members of the Church and even some leaders say they do not believe in therapy. They see it as foolishness and are very mistrustful of it. This reminds me of my father before he passed away. He was always a big fan of westerns—John Wayne movies in particular. He would often have to wait several days or even weeks before he could view a John Wayne movie on TV. We tried to persuade dad that if he purchased a VCR he could watch John Wayne movies whenever he wanted. But he was very mistrustful and suspicious of these "new fangled gadgets". In a way he was afraid of the new technology. It was something new and unknown to him. Dad received a VCR for Christmas. After a lot of persistent encouragement, dad tried his new VCR. He fell in love with it and was thrilled he could watch his favorite John Wayne movies whenever he wanted to. He experienced a lot of pleasure from his VCR before he passed away.

In many ways some leaders and members of the Church are suspicious of therapy just as my father was suspicious of VCRs. The technology is there to help in the change process but many are threatened by it. Anything unknown can be frightening. Those who try it, however, are pleasantly surprised. They find it invaluable in helping themselves and others overcome emotional problems, family and marital problems, substance abuse problems, addictions and other disorders.

Many people are fearful of therapy because they believe it will change already good people into wicked, bad people with no morals or inhibitions. This is not what therapy is all about. People do not need therapy to become more wicked. "The natural man is an enemy to God" as King Benjamin stated (Mosiah 3:19). People do not need to become engaged in therapy to follow their natural urges and carnal desires. It is as easy and natural as falling off a log to give into carnal desires and urges and thus become an "enemy of God." Therapy, the great majority of time, helps people change for the better and become whole and their absolute best selves.

For an example. let me tell you about Diane (the name has been changed to protect confidentiality). Diane is a 55-year-old woman who had experienced long-term depression and relationship problems. Even in her middle age she was stunningly beautiful. She never lacked for suitors in her life. However, her physical attraction was both a blessing and a curse to her because she often attracted the wrong kind of suitors. She was not physically abused as a child but she had a cold, critical mother. As a result, she developed a deeply ingrained belief, called a "core belief", about herself that she was not worth much and inferior to others. Despite a very successful career as an administrative assistant at the local university, she felt depressed about her life. She had been married four times. Because she did not hold herself in high esteem, she often became involved with men who were emotionally and physically abusive. They swarmed around her like bees around honey. She had never really known what a healthy, loving relationship was like. She settled for these aggressive men who literally swept her off her feet with their charming and deceitful ways. When they were abusive and demeaning to her she felt she was only getting what she deserved.

When I became involved with Diane, she was very discouraged and did not hold out much hope of ever being happy or ever being in a healthy romantic relationship. She had tried medications but they had not proven to be efficacious. I counseled with her and she worked hard to overcome her negative core beliefs and develop new positive beliefs. Gradually she started seeing herself in a different light. She began to see herself the same way others saw her as a beautiful, talented. lovely daughter of God. She also learned to set limits and boundaries. She did not tolerate any kind of abusive or disrespectful behavior. While she was involved in therapy she was attending Church, paying her tithing and striving to be temple worthy. While going through this process, she was transformed before my very eyes. She became truly happy. She also became involved with a good and honorable man who treated her with the utmost respect and love. The last time I spoke to Diane, she and her new boyfriend were discussing marriage. Diane is a great example of how the partnership of the gospel and therapy changed a person's life. Although her change was facilitated by therapy, it was ultimately a spiritual change. It occurred through the grace of God and the Holy Spirit.

Another example of a person who changed his life is Juan. Juan came in for therapy for an entirely different reason than Diane. Juan was 32 years old and had been convicted for domestic violence and court ordered to receive therapy. He was not happy at all about having to attend therapy and saw it as a complete waste of time. He did not see a need for therapy because, after all, it was his wife's fault when he lost his temper. He was from a Latin American country where violence toward family members was much more acceptable. Violence had become a way of life for Juan. I worked hard to establish a good relationship with Juan and he and I became friends. I counseled with Juan in group therapy and saw a definite softening in Juan. He dropped his suspiciousness and mistrust after several weeks and he became an eager student while in the group. He began to learn how to express feelings and solve conflicts without using violence. This way was kinder and even more effective than violence. Incidentally, Juan also started receiving the missionary discussions and attending church. The Holy Spirit started entering into Juan's life. After a few months in therapy, attending church and participation in missionary discussions he was truly changed and became much kinder and gentler. He was changed from a lion to a lamb. He did not, however, become a passive and submissive lamb. Instead he became more like a "buffed-up" lamb. He was gentle and strong, flexible and firm just as Christ.

Admittedly not all therapies are created equal. Cognitive therapy, in my experience, is much more compatible with the gospel than other therapies. Cognitive therapy is also very well researched and more effective. In the next chapter, I will be discussing the theory behind cognitive therapy.

CHAPTER 2

Cognitive Therapy

The first great psychotherapy to emerge from the twentieth century was psychoanalysis developed by Sigmund Freud. I personally do not know any practicing therapists who are purely Freudian. Psychoanalysis has not shown to be a particularly effective therapy. Most therapists, as well as the general public, have been very much influenced by it. Words like ego, defense mechanisms, repression, the unconscious, catharsis are common words in the English language. The main problem with psychoanalysis is that it does not recognize free agency. According to Freud, we are driven by instinctual drives, like the libido, and there is no place for free choice. All we can hope to do is to keep these drives in check and barely within our conscious control. I do not practice psychoanalysis but there are certainly some truths that come from psychoanalysis. For example, I believe that there is an unconscious and many of our memories, beliefs, and feelings are contained within our unconscious mind just out of reach of our conscious awareness.

The second great movement in therapy in the twentieth century was behavioral therapy, which was introduced by B.F. Skinner and others. Behavioral therapy is still very much utilized today by most therapists. It has been shown to be very effective in the treatment of many mental disorders, such as phobias and obsessive-compulsive disorder. I practice some behavioral techniques and have found them to be very effective. When I am counseling frustrated parents, for example, I talk to them about setting up a structured program of rewards and natural consequences to assist in controlling their acting out child. Here again the main problem with behavioral therapy is its failure to recognize our free agency. According to behavioral therapy, we are merely pawns to our environment and we are purely motivated by rewards and punishments.

In the 1960s a new therapy emerged called cognitive therapy and was developed primarily by Albert Ellis and Aaron Beck. I will spend some time explaining this therapy because it has been shown to be very effective in the treatment of many mental disorders and I also believe it is very compatible with the gospel as it recognizes the concept of free agency or free will. And despite some of Albert Ellis's earlier remarks, cognitive therapy is practiced by many therapists who incorporate spirituality and religion in their clinical practice without conflict.

Cognitive refers to the thinking part of our minds. According to cognitive therapists, our feelings and emotions are triggered by thoughts. Our thoughts, however, oftentimes have become automatic and habitual. We often think negatively without any conscious awareness. When we do become aware of these thoughts we usually accept them as facts without challenging them. Cognitive therapists will assist their clients in recognizing their thoughts are not facts. For example, if a person makes a mistake he will automatically think "I'm really stupid!" and he will not challenge this thought when he really should. When this type of thinking is allowed to go unchecked and unchallenged it will negatively affect a person's self-esteem and eventually his mental health

Cognitive therapy recognizes that every situation can be interpreted in more than one way. The way we interpret a situation has a profound effect on the way we feel. Again, however, people seldom question the way they are interpreting a situation. For example, a house-wife is helping her husband to remodel their house. Her husband gives her an electric drill and asks her to drill some holes in the wall. She has never used a drill before but she consents to try anyway. She has difficulty and makes some mistakes. Her husband can see she is struggling and he takes the drill from her and proceeds to drill the holes very easily and proficiently. She interprets this event in the following way. "Look how easy it was for him. I must be stupid." As often is the case with negative thoughts there is a domino effect and one negative thought leads to another negative thought. She thinks further: "I can't do anything right", "My husband must think I'm a real idiot!" Obviously there is a better way of interpreting this situation but to the housewife who is having these automatic thoughts it is not obvious at all. She could think: "I'm not stupid. I am intelligent. He just has a lot more experience than I do with electric drills." This kinder thinking could improve her self-esteem but it does not enter her mind. This kind of negative thinking is a common trap that we all fall into some times. For some people this is easily remedied with some feedback from family or friends or some time away from the situation. For others, however, this type of derogatory thinking already reinforces a negative thinking pattern. This pattern can lead to depression and anxiety if not disrupted and replaced with more realistic and positive thinking.

Albert Ellis developed a formula early in his career that explains cognitive therapy well. He says when there is an emotional upset there is first an activating event which is followed by an emotional consequence. Behavioral therapists would agree with that statement. However, Albert Ellis adds another step called our Beliefs or Self-Talk. This is how it appears in a formula:

A. Activating Event.

Plus

B. Beliefs or self-talk

Equals

C. Emotional Consequence (1)

In the example I just gave of the distraught housewife, it would appear:

A. Housewife having difficulty operating an electric drill
(Activating event)

Plus

B. "I must really be stupid" (Beliefs or self-talk)

Equals

C. Depression (Emotional consequence)

As you can see from my example, it is not really the activating event or situation that triggered her feelings or emotional consequence, it was her interpretation of the event that caused her feelings. Her belief or self-talk at the time caused her depression and not the situation itself. This is true of any situation. It is not the situations or events in our lives that ultimately determine our feelings but our own interpretation or self-talk about the event. These thoughts can occur in a nano-second but they nevertheless determine how we feel.

Through much training and practice, a person can slowly change the way he or she thinks. The first step is increasing awareness of the way we think and then realizing this way of thinking is not set in stone. There may be a more positive and realistic way of thinking. I ask clients to change their perspective and look at the activating event or situation the same way a trusted friend would look at the situation. I also ask my clients to write down the new and improved way of thinking. I encourage them to do a "Thought Record" and diagram a healthier, positive way of thinking. The above example could be diagrammed in the following way:

A. Housewife has difficulty operating a drill (Activating event)

Plus

B. "I have never operated a drill so of course I'm going to make mistakes but I am intelligent and a fast learner and I will get the hang of it" (Belief or self-talk)

Equals

C. Some mild frustration but no depression (Emotional consequence)

I have explained cognitive therapy to hundreds of my clients and I have never had any body disagree with me. It makes intuitive sense to people and they often immediately see how it applies to their own lives. They recognize how they have often gotten into a habit of negative thinking and have been accepting their negative thoughts as facts. This does not mean that it is easy to stop negative thinking. The way we think is a lifelong process and has deep roots to it. It takes hard work and practice to change our thinking but it can be done. When people change their negative way of thinking and start thinking in a more positive, rational way they feel much better and they come out of their depression. It is important to note this habit of negative thinking does not have anything to do with intelligence. I have counseled with some very intelligent people who, nevertheless, were in a habit of negative thinking. Once they began to recognize these negative thoughts and started changing them, they too felt much better.

Cognitive therapy recognizes our free agency or free will. We are not merely pawns to the events in our lives. We all have the ability to see and interpret the situation in a number of ways. We are the captains of our souls and we ultimately determine how we feel. Even when something discouraging happens and we are beset with bad fortune, we still determine how we feel by how we interpret the situation. For example, if a close family member dies, everyone would agree that is a sad event. However, even an event like that can be interpreted in a number of ways. We as L.D.S. people and other religious people look at death as a temporary separation and we believe that our loved ones go to a much more joyous place and that greatly eases our sadness and grief. Other people look at death as the end and they will never see their loved ones again. This makes their sadness and grief much worse and often more than they can bear.

When a person sins is it appropriate to feel guilt and discouragement? Does cognitive therapy say we should ever feel guilt and remorse? Yes, it is appropriate to feel guilt and remorse on occasion but not to the point of depression. To illustrate this lets say that a child lies to her parent and says she turned in her homework when in reality she did not. Her parents find out and chastise her. She feels very depressed and thinks of herself as a bad, sinful person. Diagrammed it would appear this way:

A. Child caught in a lie (Activating event)

Plus

B. "I'm a bad, sinful person" (Belief or self-talk)

Equals

C. Guilt and depression (Emotional consequence)

It is appropriate and useful for this child to feel some temporary guilt and discouragement but not depression. Depression effects our self-worth and self-esteem. Depressive thinking also tends to be all encompassing and unforgiving. We think of ourselves as worthless and no good. This is never healthy or productive and continual thoughts like these will surely cause depression. A much more appropriate and positive way of thinking for the above example would be: "I made a mistake and I am sorry for it but I know that my parents and Heavenly Father still love me. I am a good person and I will do better" This type of thinking is much more specific to the situation, realistic and forgiving. There is recognition that a mistake was made but her self-worth is preserved. Diagrammed it would appear this way:

A. Child caught in a lie (Activating event)

Plus

B. "I made a mistake and I am sorry for it but I know that

my parents and Heavenly Father still love me. I am a good person and I will do better." (Beliefs or self-talk)

Equals

C Temporary sadness and guilt but no depression. (Emotional consequence)

Sadness, temporary guilt, discouragement are normal human emotions and are at times beneficial emotions but depression is never appropriate or productive. Depression is like arsenic that can poison the soul. Guilt, on the other hand, can be a bitter medicine but ultimately leads to healing.

Many wonder where these negative thoughts come from. They seem to pop into our minds from nowhere. They actually come from what we as cognitive therapists call core beliefs. These are very deeply in grained beliefs that we all have that come primarily from our childhood and are usually unconscious. If a person has the good fortune of coming from a home that is healthy with a lot of love, then chances are he or she will also develop healthy core beliefs. If, on the other hand, a person comes from a home that is not healthy and abusive, then chances are he or she will develop unhealthy core beliefs. For example, if a person comes from a home where whenever he or she makes a mistake he is verbally abused, yelled at and called stupid, then this person develops a core belief that resembles this: "If I make a mistake then I am stupid and I need to be ashamed." This core belief then becomes like a tape recording that automatically gets turned on whenever that person makes a mistake. We are not usually aware of our core beliefs but a therapist can help a person identify his core beliefs and help that person reexamine his unhealthy beliefs. Healthy changes in thoughts lead to a healthy changes in emotion. I really enjoy seeing my clients give up old destructive core beliefs and develop new core beliefs They often blossom and become very happy- often happier and healthier than they have ever been.

I would like to give an example of this. I had a lady client by the name of Jill (names have been changed to protect confidentiality) Jill is an attractive, intelligent sister in her mid thirties and she is the mother of three children. She has a strong testimony but nevertheless suffered from chronic depression. She grew up in a home where she was physically and emotionally abused by her father. She was also in an abusive first marriage. She remarried a kinder man. He is a good husband but she remained depressed. She had developed some negative core beliefs in her childhood and these were reinforced in her first marriage. One of her core beliefs went something like this: "I can't make a mistake. If I make a mistake then I have failed and I need to be ashamed." Another core belief she had went as follows: "I am inferior to others and other people look down on me. Other people don't like being around me"

I did cognitive therapy with Jill and she started to challenge her habitual negative thoughts. Over time she began to replace her negative core beliefs with much more healthy beliefs. She replaced her old core belief about making mistakes with "When I make a mistake, it is an opportunity for growth and learning and I love myself even when I make a mistake." Another core belief I helped her develop went like this: "I am a person of high worth. I am equal to any body" Jill went through a transformation before my very eyes. She blossomed and became truly happy. In one session she related to me she had often been abused by her first husband. One day after being abused she looked in the mirror and was shocked by what she saw. She felt she looked very ugly, haggard and undesirable. She had been conditioned to think this way by the abusive men in her life combined with her negative core beliefs. After being in therapy for a while, she told me she had just recently looked at herself in the mirror and it was as if she were seeing herself for the very first time. She saw herself as a beautiful daughter of God and she really liked what she saw

As helpful as cognitive therapy is I do not believe that the change that occurred in Jill was purely cognitive or psychological. It was also a much more important spiritual change. In the twenty years that I have been a therapist I have come to recognize that change is not only a psychological and a cognitive process but also a change that occurs through the Holy Ghost. A skillful therapist can easily incorporate psychological and cognitive processes with spirituality and religion for a more complete and lasting healing that comes from God.

CHAPTER 3

Atonement

As I've grown older and hopefully a little wiser, I have gained a deeper understanding of the atonement. When I was young, I understood that the atonement was the means whereby we repent of our sins. Now I have realized that the atonement applies to much more than sin. Much of what I have learned about the atonement was revealed to me by the book <u>The Broken Heart</u> by Elder Bruce Hafen of the Seventy. I remember reading late into the night and being enthralled by this book. I received a personal witness from the Holy Ghost that the teachings of this book are true. My eyes were opened to the broader scope of the atonement.

As Elder Hafen explained, and I have learned for myself, the atonement applies to any kind of adversity we are struggling with. Part of the purpose of this life is to suffer. I do not believe that the Lord intends for our suffering to be a permanent condition and for it to be our lot in life. But we are all faced with adversity in life whether that be diabetes, cancer, a learning disability, an addiction or depression. God places these challenges in our lives as learning experiences and he expects us to overcome these challenges with his help and guidance. We are to become happy in spite of our infirmities and afflictions. For as Lehi said: "Men are that they might have joy" (2 Nephi 2:25). The *Book of Mormon* offers so much consolation for those who are suffering from depression, anxiety, and any kind of mental or physical disorder. The following two passages of scripture from the *Book of Mormon* are examples of this consolation:

"And he cometh into the world that he may save all men if they will hearken unto his voice; for behold, he suffereth the pains of all men, yea, the pains of every living creature, both men, women and children, who belong to the family of Adam." (2 Nephi 9:20)

"And he will go forth suffering pains and afflictions and temptations of every kind; and this that the word might be fulfilled that saith that he taketh upon him the pains and sicknesses of his people. And he will take upon him death, that he may loose the bands of death which bind his people; and he will take upon him their infirmities, that his bowels may be filled with mercy, according the flesh, that he may know, according to the flesh, how to succor his people according to their infirmities." (Alma 7:11-12)

I have explained this principle to clients that it is through the atonement that they will be cured from their depression, anxiety, addiction or whatever emotional or mental problem they are suffering with. They are usually surprised. I was unaware of this principle myself until recent years. This is certainly not something I learned in graduate school. However, as my understanding of the gospel and my faith in Jesus Christ have deepened, the power and the universality of the atonement has been impressed on me. This has only made me more grateful to the Savior for his marvelous gift of the atonement.

Another concept that I have come to appreciate in recent years is how the atonement is the main vehicle of change in our lives. As we grow up as children in this very imperfect world, we become by nature carnal, sensual, and devilish. As King Benjamin said "The natural man is an enemy to God" (Mosiah 3:19) I just had my first grandson four months ago. As I gaze at that beautiful baby, I do not believe that my infant grandson is by nature devilish, carnal and sensual. Babies are born whole, complete and without sin. However, as a consequence of growing up in a telestial world we become by nature carnal, sinful, and sensual. This idea is similar to what some famous psychiatrists have taught. Carl Jung, for instance, said that children are born whole but develop "masks" or "false selves" as they mature and grow up in imperfect homes. These "masks" lead to mental and emotional problems. One of the tasks of psychotherapy is to help people take off their "masks" and discover their authentic selves and become whole once again. In a similar way, through the atonement, we can change and throw off our carnal selves. We can discover who we really are. We are literally children of God who are good and more precious than diamonds and rubies.

As scriptural basis for what I am proposing, I give these references that through the atonement we can change and become "new creatures."

"And now because of the covenant that ye have made ye shall become the children of Christ, his sons and his daughters; for behold this day he hath spiritually begotten you; for ye say that your hearts have been *changed* through faith on his name; therefore ye are born of him and have become his sons and his daughters" (Mosiah 5:7)

"And behold, he (Alma) preached the word unto your fathers, and a mighty *change* was also wrought in their hearts, and they humbled themselves and put their trust in the true and living God. And behold, they were faithful unto the end; therefore they were saved. And now behold, I ask of you my brethren of the Church, have ye spiritually been born of God? Have ye received his image in your countenances? Have ye experienced this mighty *change* in your hearts?" (Alma 5:13-14)

"Therefore if any man be in Christ, he is a *new creature*: old things are passed away; behold, all things are become new" (2 Cor 5:17)

A couple of years ago, I had as a client a lovely, elegant and intelligent 56 year old lady by the name of Anne, who had suffered from depression for many years. She had been in therapy before with little success. She was willing to engage in therapy again but with little hope that therapy would help. She was a woman with a strong testimony and great faith. I did cognitive therapy with her and I also explained to her that her recovery would be spiritual in nature. Ultimately, she would be cured of her depression through the atonement. She responded well to cognitive therapy and after several sessions her depression subsided and she was happier than she had ever been. When I asked her what had made the difference in her life, I expected her to say it was her wonderful therapist and cognitive therapy. I was pleasantly surprised when she said the factor that had most contributed to her recovery was God and the Holy Ghost. When cognitive therapy had been combined with her great faith in Jesus Christ, she made great strides.

I do fervently believe that clients who change dramatically in therapy and become "new creatures" ultimately change through the Holy Ghost and the power of the atonement. However, therapy plays an important role in recovery and facilitates this spiritual recovery.

CHAPTER 4

Tying it together

I regard this as the most important chapter in this book. This is where I attempt to show that the gospel of Jesus Christ and therapy do complement each other. Cognitive therapy and the gospel have the same goal to bring joy and happiness to mankind. Cognitive therapy, in particular, was revealed, as is all truth, through the Holy Ghost. All great discoveries, whether it be the discovery of penicillin by Alexander Fleming or the double helix and the structure of DNA by John Watson, were revealed through the power of the Holy Ghost. Albert Ellis and Aaron Beck were the main originators of cognitive therapy back in the 1950s and 1960s. I believe they were both inspired by God to develop this therapy as it has brought happiness to many people. Admittedly, Albert Ellis is an avowed atheist; but, whether he will admit it or not he was inspired by the Holy Ghost to develop this therapy! As it states in our thirteenth article of faith: "...if there is anything virtuous, lovely, or good report or praise-worthy, we seek after these things." Cognitive therapy certainly is praiseworthy and of good report Competent therapists should study it seriously and apply it for the benefit of their clients. Multiple studies have shown it to be effective in the treatment of depression, anxiety, phobias and other mental disorders.

How does cognitive therapy and the gospel work together to bring relief from suffering? I will answer this question in this chapter. Depression and other mental disorders are terrible and are often worse than physical disorders because depression and other mental disorders affect our minds. As a person who suffered from depression and anxiety many years ago and as someone who has talked to hundreds of people who suffer from it, I can attest that depression, obsessions, phobias, and other mental problems can make our minds into a living hell. The sufferer feels trapped in a prison he cannot escape. . He needs the help of caring professional people, family and Jesus Christ to unlock the door of this prison.

Depression is like a dense fog or "mist of darkness" as stated in Lehi's dream. Many people are lost in this fog or mist. They wander about aimlessly, are confused and are looking for a way out. One of the most awful parts of being lost in this fog is that it is hard to see the light. It is hard to see the light of Christ in this fog and it is hard to feel the warmth of God's love in this fog. Many people doubt the existence of God and Christ in this fog of depression. Others still believe in God while they are lost in this fog but they believe they are not worthy of God's love. They may believe they have committed some unforgivable sins and are not worthy of God's love. They may also believe that this suffering they are experiencing is their punishment in life for the many mistakes they have committed. They may see it as their lot in life that God intends for them to suffer for the rest of their lives. I know this is not God's intention. He does not want any of his beloved children to suffer forever and He provides a way out of the darkness. We know the way out of the fog is to grab hold of the iron rod. The iron rod, as we have been told in the scriptures, is the word of God. I am bold enough to suggest that the rod of iron may also represent something else. It may also represent professional treatment and therapy. A combination of the gospel and professional treatment can lead us out of the dense fog of depression and other mental and emotional illnesses.

I explained the basic concepts of cognitive therapy in chapter two. The principles of cognitive therapy are easy for most people to comprehend. It makes intuitive sense to most people and they grasp these concepts readily. That does not mean these concepts are easy to implement. Clients must work and practice to implement the principles of cognitive therapy I always give homework assignments for clients to work on between sessions. The clients who practice the principles and do the homework benefit the most from therapy. Recently, I was explaining cognitive therapy to a 21-year old returned missionary who will be called Jeff. He suffers from severe obsessions and depression. Jeff is a good, faithful man who has a strong testimony and is serious scholar of the scriptures. After a particularly good session with Jeff, he remarked he knew that the things we had talked about were true. He knew it by the power of the Holy Ghost as the Spirit had testified to him of its truthfulness. He is making good progress and is coming out of his depression and his obsessions. We both thank God for cognitive therapy and the concepts borrowed from other therapies that have helped him.

I have often felt the Spirit during and after a good session. It is a similar feeling that I get in fast and testimony meeting. This is one of the marks of good therapy and an indicator that the therapy is of God. It edifies and uplifts. In *Doctrine and Covenants* 50:22 it states:

"Wherefore, he that preacheth and he that receiveth understand one another, and both are edified and rejoice together"

This scripture refers specifically to missionary work; but, in a very similar way, good therapy works in the same fashion. This is one of the ways a person can tell if therapy is helping and if it is of God. If that peaceful, warm feeling is present in the therapy session then the Holy Ghost is also present with its healing power. When clients do not feel warm, peaceful feelings and if it does not edify then it is not good therapy. It is also not of God. Anything of God uplifts and brings feelings of peace and joy. The Spirit is stronger in some sessions than others but it should nevertheless be present. Therefore, if you do not *feel* good about your therapy then therapy is not helping and you should discuss this with your therapist and possibly discontinue therapy with this therapist. .

There is one caveat to the above point. Sometimes it is necessary to go back into a person's past and discuss some painful memories, like sexual abuse for example. This can be very painful and difficult for a client. This is necessary for the healing to commence. It is controversial just how much these painful memories need to be discussed. However, I do not believe these memories should be dwelt upon extensively and the client should feel good about the overall course of therapy

Another good test for therapy is to pray about it. I often encourage clients to pray about their sessions. I encourage them to put Moroni's promise to the test about our therapy just as if they were praying about the truthfulness of the *Book of Mormon* as stated in Moroni 10:4-5. I ask them to pray about what we have discussed in our session and ask God for a spiritual witness that what has been discussed is true. After all, as stated in Moroni 10:5 "And by the power of the Holy Ghost you may know the truth of all things." For something as important as therapy and restructuring a person's way of thinking, it is critical that a client pray for a witness from God that the concepts and ideas presented in therapy are true.

Another litmus test for good therapy concerns our values. An ethical therapist would never ask a client to go against his or her values. I do not believe that LDS members should fear going to non-LDS therapists but those therapists should respect your values and beliefs. If, for instance, a therapist were to suggest to you that there is nothing morally wrong with masturbation and encourages the practice then that therapist is not respecting your values and you should terminate with that particular therapist. If a therapist were counseling you to get an abortion then it would be wise to stop seeing that therapist. A therapist does not have to share every one of your values to be of benefit to you, but the therapist should respect your values and not impose his or her values on you.

Therapy and the atonement work together to relieve suffering and bring happiness. One of the purposes of therapy is to make the "unconscious conscious." As I mentioned in chapter two, the automatic thoughts that people have are barely perceptible. Thoughts happen habitually and people barely notice these thoughts. As I said before, its just like a tape recording being turned on in our brains. Making a mistake, for instance, turns on a tape recording in our mind: "I'm so stupid! I can't believe I did that. I can't do anything right". In cognitive therapy, clients slow down their thinking and examine these automatic thoughts. I ask clients to write down their thoughts when they are feeling depressed or anxious and to carefully analyze them. I ask them to do "Thought Records" and teach them to rationally and objectively analyze these thoughts and look for more positive interpretations of the situation.

As I also mentioned in Chapter 2, our automatic thoughts originate from our core beliefs. These core beliefs are unconscious and buried deep within our psyches. It usually takes the help of a therapist to make these core beliefs conscious. For example, a therapist can help a client become conscious of a core belief like: "I cannot make mistakes. If I do make a mistake then I have failed and need to be ashamed." A therapist will help that client develop a more healthy belief like: "Mistakes are opportunities for growth and learning and I still love myself even when I make a mistake" In the uncovering of these unconscious beliefs, the atonement plays an important part in recovery. After these dysfunctional beliefs have been uncovered, the atonement can heal us. I would like to offer the following analogy. When I was a young boy there was a commercial for "*Mentholatum* Deep Heating Rub" I remember my father using this odoriferous substance for his sore muscles, and the whole house knew when dad was using his *Mentholatum* too. This magical gel would seep down into sore muscles and bring relief and healing to aching muscles and joints. Therapy and the atonement work in the same fashion. After therapy has uncovered unconscious beliefs, then the atonement can seep and penetrate the recesses of our mind and cure us. The atonement and the Holy Ghost are the healing "balm of Gilead" that can cure our dysfunctional patterns of thought and make us whole. However, it takes the help of a therapist or another skilled person to uncover the wound and clean it out and then the atonement can work through the power of the Holy Ghost.

I would like to conclude this chapter by summarizing how to tell the difference between good and bad therapy and how to tell if therapy is working with the spirit of the Holy Ghost:

1. Does therapy uplift, edify and feel right? If it does not then it is not of God and is not helping and may even do

some harm.

2. Pray about your therapy and ask Heavenly Father for a witness that the therapy concepts and techniques are true. If you do not receive a spiritual witness then it is not of God.

3. Does the therapist ask you to go against your values and beliefs or question your values and beliefs. An ethical therapist would not do that and you should immediately seek therapy elsewhere.

In the next four chapters I will be discussing four core beliefs that are particularly bothersome. The majority of clients suffering from depression and other mental disorders have at least one and sometimes all of these particular core beliefs. LDS people and other members of conservative religions are especially vulnerable to these beliefs. I have come up with the acronym: **PENS** or in other words: Perfectionism, Excessive responsibility, Neglecting our own needs and Sagging self-worth. Just like pens on a farm keep livestock and animals penned in and contained, these **PENS** contain us and stop us from experiencing joy and happiness and reaching our true potential.

Spiritual Therapy

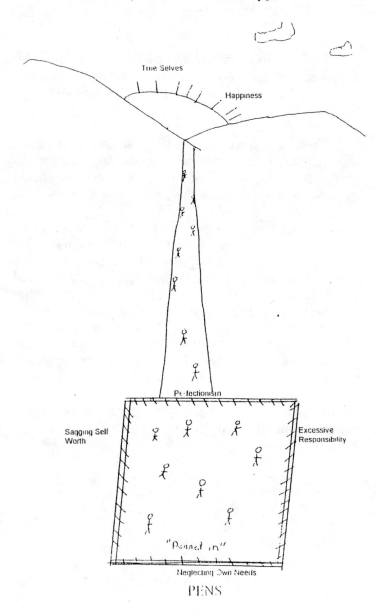

True Selves

Happiness

Perfectionism

Sagging Self
Worth

Excessive
Responsibility

"Penned in"

Neglecting Own Needs

PENS

CHAPTER 5

Perfectionism

Perfectionism goes something like this: " I cannot make a mistake and if I do make a mistake then I have failed and need to be ashamed of myself." Individuals who have this core belief are full of shame because they often feel that God is also ashamed of them and could not possibly love them. This core belief, like most core beliefs, originates in childhood. In dysfunctional homes where there is physical and emotional abuse, mistakes are severely punished and children learn that it is definitely not okay to make mistakes.

Even in otherwise good, loving homes this core belief can develop. For instance, if a child brings home a report card of almost all A's but her parents only notice the B's then the child could get the message: "I expect perfection. What's the matter with you?" In another example, a child, who has an otherwise good basketball game, but misses the final basket that could have won the game, may get criticism from one or both parents; or, if not criticism, then he may get silence, which also speaks volumes and in effect says "I'm disappointed in you." In some homes where older siblings are high achievers, like star athletes, valedictorians, etc.; there is tremendous pressure on younger siblings to live up to those very high standards. Even with parents who are very supportive and loving, the child feels tremendous pressure to live up to his siblings achievements. If they do not, they feel they have let their family down and themselves down. Anything less than perfection is thought to be not good enough because, after all, my older brother or sister did it.

I have counseled with some outstanding youth in my career but who have this negative perfectionistic core belief and who suffer from depression, anxiety, shame and unnecessary guilt. They may feel so much shame that they will not even confide in their parents or priesthood leaders. They start to expect that they are going to fail and give up hope. I have also counseled with some outstanding returned missionaries who are committing some relatively minor sins and moral offenses but are ruthless with themselves and see themselves as moral degenerates. They believe God cannot possibly love them since they loath and hate themselves

People who think this way do not understand God's plan and do not understand the atonement. God sent us to earth knowing that we would all make many mistakes including sin. He expects us to learn from these mistakes and he has provided a way through the atonement to correct these mistakes and become cleansed. To quote from Elder Bruce Hafen:

"There will always be mistakes in each phase of the learning process from those awkward beginning stages toward the tentativeness of intermediacy and finally the confidence of advanced studies...The crucial question in these experiences is not whether they will come along, as all of us encounter them; rather the question is whether we can learn from our early mistakes. If we can, even if only gradually, we will learn to prize the good. Our maturation will be underway. If we cannot, we will move into larger-scale trans-gressions. For now we are considering a basic perspective on all negative human experience, including adversity and inadequacy, miscalculations and care-lessness, along with deliberate and willful transgression. All are part of opposition and mortality, and all can be a source of growth and development, depending upon our response to them . . . life is a learning laboratory. Without this understanding, we may miss some of life's vital lessons." (1)

Mistakes, including sin, must be looked as an opportunity for learning and growth. We cannot despise ourselves and lose confidence when we do make mistakes. God does not stop loving us when we make mistakes and neither should we. I used to be a student of near-death experiences and I read several books about them. I found them to be fascinating and a confirmation of my testimony of the gospel. Many people describe entering an incredibly beautiful and brilliant white light when they die. Some people indicate this is Christ and they are entering into His presence. They all remark that when they enter this other-worldly light, they feel nothing but pure love. This love is like nothing they have previously experienced and is extremely joyful. It reminds me of Lehi's dream of the fruit of the tree of life. This exceedingly white fruit is the love of God and Lehi says when he partook of this fruit his soul was filled with "exceedingly great joy" and was "desirable above all other fruit" 1Nephi 8:12. Many people when they enter this beautiful light are given a life review. They are allowed to see all their mistakes, sins and selfish acts. However, they still continue to feel the unconditional love from the being of light even when they are reviewing their mistakes and sins. He never stops loving them. They are allowed to judge themselves but they never stop feeling the pure love from the being of light. I believe these near death experiences are real and represent God's unconditional love toward us. It is the same kind of love we should have for ourselves. We should have unconditional love toward ourselves as God does and simply learn from our mistakes. It is appropriate to feel guilt and remorse at times but we should not stop loving ourselves.

Taking responsibility for our mistakes is also important. We should not try to blame others or circumstances when we do make mistakes. Taking responsibility for our mistakes can be very freeing. We do not have to worry about trying to cover up our mistake. Great athletes are a good example of this. My son has a Nike poster in his room from Michael Jordan and it reads: "I've missed more than 9000 shots in my career. I've lost almost 300 games. Twenty-six times I've been trusted to take the game winning shot and missed. I've failed over and over and over again in my life. And that is why I succeed." The great Michael Jordan does not berate himself when he misses a shot. He uses it as a springboard to try harder until he succeeds. I remember the great forward for the Utah Jazz, Karl Malone, was playing in a playoff game against L.A Lakers several years ago. He had an absolutely horrible game and only made 3 out of 19 field goal attempts. After the game, when he was being interviewed he did not try to excuse himself. He took full responsibility for his poor performance. There was no dropping in his self-worth or confidence at all and he promised he would come back stronger than ever. As he predicted, in his very next game he came back with a vengeance and had one of his very best games ever and scored over 30 points. We could all learn from the example of these great athletes. The truly outstanding athletes do not always excel but they continue to have confidence in themselves when they are not doing well and they push forward until they do succeed.

I learned this lesson unexpectedly several years ago. I am not a big video game player but several years ago I did get hooked on a video game called <u>Pitfall</u>. The object of this game was to go though underground tunnels until you rescue the princess. Along the way are numerous pitfalls and death traps: bats, scorpions, underground rivers and the like. Every time I made a mistake and was killed, I had to go back to the beginning and try again. I was literally killed a thousand times. Each time, however, I would get a little further until finally, at two o'clock in the morning, I made it all the way through the tunnel and rescued the princess. I was exultant. I was cheering and yelling for joy. My wife thought I had gone crazy. Afterwards, I thought this is a perfect analogy for life. I could have given up on myself and told myself I am a failure and no good at this game. However, I did not say that to myself but pressed forward even with my thousands of mistakes until I had obtained the prize. In athletics this prize would be a championship. In the game of life this prize would be eternal life.

Another useful way to look at mistakes is to take a problem-solving approach. Instead of belittling ourselves and condemning ourselves when we make a mistake, we need to take a problem-solving approach. I learned this from my older brother a few years ago. He is an electrical engineer and he offered to upgrade our computer for us. We took him up on the offer. He started working on our computer but had more difficulty than he anticipated and he ran into snafu after snafu. It took him much longer than he had anticipated and he had to start over several times. Finally, he did finish upgrading the computer and it worked great. I was amazed that he never got angry or upset. He kept correcting mistakes and problems calmly and resolutely until he had corrected them all. I asked him how he managed to stay so calm. I probably would have been pulling my hair out. He said that engineering is nothing but problem-solving and this project was very typical of his work. Engineers expect to make mistakes and expect to confront problems. They don't get discouraged. They just keep problem solving until they have figured it out and accomplished what they set out to do. I tease and joke with my brother that in the next life there will be no need for engineers and that we will all be social workers. He insists we will be building new worlds and have to be engineers. In this one respect, I have to admit we should all be like engineers and take a problem-solving approach to life.

Do all these analogies and examples I have given apply to sin? Admittedly, making a mistake in upgrading a computer or playing a video game is not the same as committing adultery, lying, stealing or committing any sin. It is appropriate to have guilt when we sin. However, I believe the same principles apply. We should still look at sin as learning opportunities. It is useful to differentiate between guilt and shame. Guilt is remorse and sadness when we sin and is very motivating. Guilt can also be a great teacher. Guilt is like a mother who is pushing a dallying child out the door and off to school. Guilt points us in the right direction. Guilt should be temporary and ends when we have fully repented. Shame is very different and is not useful or productive as guilt can be. Shame should be avoided. Shame is more like a whip that inflicts injury. Shame can also last forever. Shame means when we sin or make a mistake, we devalue ourselves and think of ourselves as worthless and no good. It leads to depression and is self-defeating.

It is important to remember that ultimately the way we overcome sin is through the grace of Jesus Christ and his atonement. We need to pray with our whole souls to be forgiven of that sin and ask the Lord to give us that sweet peace of conscience that indicates we have been forgiven. Sometimes this involves confession to a priesthood authority as well. As stated in 2 Nephi 25:23 "for we know that it is by grace that we are saved, after all we can do."

I encourage clients to have a core belief like this. "Mistakes are opportunities for growth and are inevitable and necessary for our learning. I love myself even when I make a mistake" This is a whole new way of viewing mistakes for many people. There is no place for shame. We have no loss of confidence and self-esteem when we do not do things just right. We avoid the "all or nothing thinking" that is so common among depressed people. "If I do not do everything perfectly, I am a failure." All or nothing thinking is a tool of Lucifer's that leads us to give up.

The best way to strengthen a new core belief is to act on it. It involves interrupting those automatic thoughts. It involves "catching ourselves" when we think negatively and replacing it with our new, kinder way of thinking. This is a very conscious and deliberate process. I often encourage clients to write down their negative thoughts in a "Thought Record." This can be as simple as drawing a line down the middle of a sheet of paper and, on the left side of the paper, writing down the negative, irrational, automatic way of thinking and, on the other side of the paper, writing the new positive, rational way of thinking. I encourage clients to look at their mistakes or goof ups in the same way a good friend would look at the mistake and to write down this more benevolent way of thinking on the right side of the paper. They usually feel better after they do this. A formal way of doing a thought record is to complete "The Daily Record of Dysfunctional Thought" developed by Dr. Beck and his associates. (2) On the next page is an example of a formal thought record:

Acting on a new core belief can involve other things as well. It may mean taking more risks and being willing to make mistakes if that is what it means to progress and grow. It could mean freely admitting when we make a mistake and, without any shame at all, asking for assistance without trying to hide our mistakes. Just as important is to pray to Heavenly Father and ask him to make the new core belief our new way of thinking.

THOUGHT RECORD

<u>Event</u>

I blew my diet
and had two
pieces of pie
at the ward
party

<u>Cognition</u>

What's the use?
I just don't have
what it takes. I'll
always be a fat
slob.

<u>Feeling</u>

Depressed

<u>Other possible interpretation</u>

I splurged tonight but
overall I have been doing
well. I deserve a treat
once in a while. Tomorrow
I'll get right back on my
eating plan.

CHAPTER 6

Excessive Responsibility

Obviously taking responsibility for our actions and mistakes is an admirable trait. It is essential for our growth and progress. Criminals and anti-social personalities do not take responsibility for their actions and this prevents them from growing and maturing. For such individuals, it is always somebody else's fault they are in the predicament that they are in. "It's my wife's fault", "It's my parents' fault", "The police in this town just have it in for me" are some of the excuses one commonly hears from these people. Another category of people are on the other end of the continuum, who not only take responsibility for their own sins and mistakes but they take responsibility for everybody else's as well. I sometimes refer to these people as "guilt sponges". If there is any guilt to be had they quickly soak it up whether it rightfully belongs to them or not. I am a fan of <u>Ziggy</u> comics. I clipped a comic where Ziggy is lying on a psychiatrist's coach and is telling the psychiatrist: "I don't know if I'm an egocentric or a guilt ridden paranoid but every time there's an eclipse, I think I caused it" This reminds me so much of many of my clients. If there were an eclipse of the sun, they would somehow feel responsible for it!

ZIGGY   **BY TOM WILSON**

Dr. Scott Peck in his enlightening book: <u>The Road Less Traveled</u> refers to these two categories of mental health clients as the "neurotics" and "character disorders." I have found this generalization true. The type of people who voluntarily come to mental health agencies are typically the "worried wells" or "neurotics" who worry about whether they have done something wrong. They readily assume guilt and blame for problems in their marriages, jobs or any other aspect of their lives. They are usually very high functioning, wonderful people but they can often be seen wringing their hands over their supposed indiscretions. They spend sleepless nights worrying about who they have offended and what they should have done differently. Character disordered clients, on the other hand, are usually court ordered clients who really do not know why they have been ordered into treatment. They worry little and have no guilt. According to them, it was my wife' fault or my parent's fault that I behaved as I did. It is amazing to me that the "neurotics" and "character-disordered" often find and marry each other! (1)

People with the excessive responsibility core belief have a belief something like this: "If something goes wrong, it's my fault and I must fix it" Like perfectionism, children who grow up in abusive homes often develop this belief. They are often made to feel like it is always their fault whenever something goes wrong in their families. These irresponsible, abusive parents often blame and criticize their own children rather than take responsibility for their own sins. However, in otherwise good families, this core belief can also develop. I have noticed that the oldest daughter often is vulnerable to this belief. Much responsibility is put on these daughters to care for their younger siblings. Whenever a younger sibling misbehaves these oldest children are made to feel responsible. "I told you to watch them and I am holding you accountable" is the reproof they often hear from their parents when a younger sibling willfully disobeys. Guilt is an all too common emotion for these particular people. It seems their whole motivation for any thing they do is guilt and shame based.

It is interesting how irresponsible, character disordered people often seek out these overly respon-sible people. It is as if criminals, many alcoholics, drug addicts and character disordered individuals are wearing radar and are instantly drawn to these excessively responsible, potential victims. They may be their own parents, soon to be girlfriends and wives, co-workers or bosses. Once they are in these relationships, they are only too happy to bestow all the guilt and responsibility for their mistakes and sins onto these neurotic people. Otherwise, the character disordered people could not survive. I remember Ruth, a 42-year old devoted mother and wife, who was severely exploited by her sons. She had 19 and 18 year old sons who still lived at home. They did not work or go to school and both were addicted to alcohol and drugs. Their behavior was often outrageous but they had their mother wrapped around their proverbial little fingers. All they had to do was to intimate that it was their mothers fault and she was quick to excuse their behavior. She unwittingly became an "enabler" to her sons' addictions and irresponsible behavior. This made it possible for them to continue living in her home living these very anti-social lifestyles. Ruth needless to say suffered from severe unnecessary guilt and shame, anxiety, and depression.

Elder Richard D. Scott has spoken of these parents, like Ruth, who have wayward children and who are so driven with guilt and shame. He advises such parents to:

"Keep perspective. When you have done all that you can reasonably do, rest the burden in the hands of the Lord. When I take a small pebble and place it directly in front of my eye, it takes on the appearance of a mighty boulder. It is all I can see. It becomes all-consuming—like the problems of a loved one that affect our lives every waking moment. When the things you realistically can do to help are done, leave the matter in the hands of the Lord and worry no more. Do not feel guilty because you cannot do more. Do not waste your energy on useless worry. The Lord will take the pebble that fills your vision and cast it down among the challenges you will face in your eternal progress. It will then be seen in perspective. . . . Some who have overcome serious sin in their lives blame themselves because of that prior disobedience when a loved one does not respond as desired. Such promptings are from Satan, not from the Lord. Alma could help his son, Corianton, because Alma spoke from a position of strength and knowing that his own sins had been entirely forgiven through repentance." (2)

What parent cannot recall serious mistakes he or she made in the raising of his children. I believe I have been a generally good parent but I can clearly recall some glaring mistakes I made with my children. Despite these mistakes there must come a point when our children reach the age of accountability and they are now responsible for their own lives. To paraphrase our second article of faith: "We believe that men (and women) will be punished for their own sins and not for our parents transgressions" As painful as it is, we must sometimes as parents stand back and watch our children struggle and suffer from the consequences of their own behavior. Sometimes we may actually have to help facilitate this suffering. I know some parents who recently had to press charges and testify against their own drug-addicted son who had been stealing from them. I know this was extremely painful for this couple to do but was absolutely necessary for their son's own good.

One of the best examples of responsible parenting is from the parable of the prodigal son. The story is a very familiar one. A son decided he wanted to have his inheritance and demanded it of his father. The father reluctantly gave it to him and his son took this money and had the time of his life in "riotous living" In today's parlance, he spent his money on drugs, alcohol, pornography, prostitution or any of a number of evil endeavors. Eventually his sins caught up to him and he ran out of money and was forced to take a very demeaning and humbling job feeding swine. He was hungry and suffering. He then "came to himself" and decided he needed to repent and return to his father and beg for forgiveness. He was ready to start living responsibly. From a distance, his father saw him coming and ran to meet him and embraced him and loved him. He accepted his son back with no reservation. One of the main points or lessons of this parable is forgiveness and repentance but an important lesson for parents is often not noticed. ; Although the father of the prodigal son certainly sorrowed for his son, there is no indication that he blamed himself. He also did not search the countryside trying to find his son so he could rescue him. He allowed his son to go through this necessary suffering until his son "came to himself", humbled himself and repented. (3) As parents, we should allow our children to suffer the consequences of their own behavior and not blame ourselves for our children's mistakes and disobedience. Especially as children grow into adolescence and adulthood they should be held accountable for their own actions.

The negative consequences then for the core belief of excessive responsibility is continuous and unnecessary guilt, shame, depression and anxiety. We also run the risk of becoming enablers and rescuers of others. The new core belief I suggest for my clients is "When something goes wrong I will not automatically blame myself. I will look to the cause and decide if I am in anyway responsible. If I am not responsible, I will protect my integrity and not allow others to blame me for their mistakes and problems". Of course, we may sometimes choose to help others' with their problems but we must not own their problems for them. It must remain their mistake or problem and they are ultimately responsible for their own lives.

After clients learn to interrupt the automatic thoughts and really analyze a problem or negative event, it may become very apparent they are not in any way responsible for a problem or negative event. Dr. Aaron Beck calls this process reattribution or "de-responsibilitizing" when clients think about other causes besides themselves that led to a mistake or problem. (4) They then can let go of the useless guilt and shame. However, other times the answer may not be that obvious and a person may wonder how much of the responsibility for a problem belongs to them. Greenburger and Padesky in their book <u>Mind Over Mood</u> developed the concept of responsibility pie and this has been a very helpful tool to many of my clients to decide how much responsibility and guilt belongs to them for a problem and how much belongs to others. (5) I will illustrate this with an example. Jane, age 55, is a very faithful, intelligent and appealing Relief Society president. She is a very high functioning individual but she suffers from endless guilt and depression. She has an elderly woman in her ward who had become very dependent on her. This elderly sister has health problems and frequently asked Jane to take her to doctor appointments, pharmacy, and so forth. For some reason, she would not ask her own family but would instead ask Jane for assistance. This elderly sister had a heart attack and was hospitalized. She was in intensive care and Jane felt terribly guilty and ashamed that she had not been available to this sister to get her to the hospital. She felt personally responsible for her heart attack. We decided to diagram this in a pie chart and decide how much of the responsibility actually did belong to Jane. We decided that half of the responsibility for her health problems and transportation had to belong to the elderly sister herself—at least 50%. This elderly sister had abdicated much of the responsibility for caring for herself onto other people, like Jane. Another 40% belonged to her family, which had been somewhat negligent in their duties of caring for her. Two percent belonged to her home teachers. Two percent belonged to her visiting teachers. Two percent belonged to the bishop and two percent belonged to her neighbors. That left two percent of the responsibility for this woman's health problems and transporting her to her doctor, the hospital and other appointments with her as the Relief Society president - a mere sliver of the pie. Diagrammed on the following page, it looked this way:

Responsibility Pie

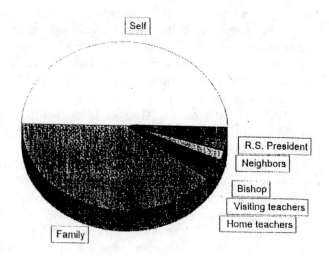

In the past, this dear, hardworking, compass-sionate Relief Society president wanted to eat the whole pie of responsibility for this sister's health. She often felt more responsible for this elderly sister's medical problems and welfare than her family and the sister herself. Completing a responsibility pie helped her to let go of unnecessary guilt and shame.

Letting go is a process that we must all go through to get rid of unnecessary guilt and shame. Sometimes letting go can be very quick and easy with little thought and deliberation. Other times it may be a very long and difficult process. Letting go of responsi-bility for a son's or daughter's drug problem, for instance, or even a family member's suicide may take quite some time. I believe it is appropriate to ask the Lord for help in this process of letting go. I offer this poem that I think speaks well about what it takes to let go.

Let Go

To "let go" does not mean to stop caring,
it means I can't do it for someone else
To "let go" is not to cut myself off,
it's the realization that I can't control another.
To "let go "is not to enable,
but to allow learning from natural consequence
To "let go" is to admit powerlessness
which means the outcome is not in my hands.
To "let go" is not to try and change or blame another,
it's to make the most of myself.
To "let go" is not to "care for"
but to "care about"
To "let go" is not to judge,
but to allow another to be a human being.
To "let go" is to not be in the middle, arranging all the outcomes,

but to allow others to affect their own destinies.
To "let go" is not to be protective,
it's to permit another to face reality.
To "let go" is not to defy,
but to accept.
To "let go" is not to nag, scold, or argue,
but instead to search out my own shortcomings and
correct them.
To "let go" is not to adjust everything to my desires,
but to try to become what I dream I can be.
To "let go" is not to regret the past,
but to grow and live for the future.
To "let go" is to fear less and love more.

Anonymous.

To strengthen the new belief about responsibility may often require being able to say "no" to people when they are asking too much and wanting us to do something they could very well do for themselves or their family could do for them. It also means establishing good boundaries and protecting our integrity. This chapter naturally leads to the next chapter about taking care of our own needs.

CHAPTER 7

Neglecting our own needs

This core belief is very common in the Church as well as among many other Christian people. It goes like this: "Other peoples' needs come first. My feelings and needs always come last." This attitude is particularly prevalent among women. This core belief is one of the main reasons why depression is so much more common among women than it is among men. (1) Women are conditioned differently than men and are taught at a very young age to be caregivers. Girls are given dolls to care for and boys are given toy trucks and guns to have fun with. Heavenly Father intended for us to have different roles and He intends that women be the main caregivers and men to be the providers and breadwinners. But, many women forget about the obligation to care for themselves while we men sometimes go in the opposite direction and become too selfish and too concerned about satisfying our pleasures and wants.

I would like to describe a typical scenario. A father and husband comes home from work. After giving his wife and kids a kiss he kicks up his feet. His wife is frantically running around trying to clean up piles of dirty laundry and dishes and get dinner ready at the same time. Her husband meanwhile is reading the newspaper or maybe watching sports on ESPN without any guilt whatsoever. He is hardly even aware of what his wife is doing. However, even when it does slow down a bit and the wife has a little time to relax she is busy folding clothes or mending pants or shirts while she is "relaxing" on the coach watching TV. Does this sound familiar? I think this is more or less true in the majority of families. Women work us under the table but we men do not seem to mind at all. Somehow a balance needs to be struck between these two extremes. Both work and relaxation are equally important and should not be focused on solely to the exclusion of the other.

I remember a few years ago working with a woman by the name of Joan. She was in her mid-forties but looked older than her chronological age. She appeared very haggard, run down and poorly groomed. She had some serious health problems including diabetes, hypertension, and high cholesterol. Her doctor warned her if she did not make some adjustments in her life and quickly she was headed for a heart attack or stroke. She worked in a stressful job in a dentist's office. She then came home to a large family and did almost all the housework, cooking and child care. Her husband and children, as in many families, took her for granted and gave her little support. She also suffered from clinical depression and anxiety. She, of course, had this core belief that other peoples' needs always come first. Even during those rare times when she did have time to relax she felt guilty and had to keep working virtually all the time. She is not atypical of many women in the Church.

One of my favorite scriptures is Mosiah 4:27 "And see that all these things are done in wisdom and order: for it is not requisite that man should run faster than he has strength." I would like to add it is not requisite for a woman to run faster than she has strength either. How do we know when we are running faster than we have strength? We develop physical and emotional symptoms. Continual stress triggers such physical symptoms as headaches, high blood pressure, stomach aches, ulcers, eczema, heart palpitations, etc.; In addition to the core belief mentioned above, stress is certainly a major contributor to depression and its symptoms i.e. tiredness, crying spells, sleep disturbance—either sleeping too much or sleeping too little, appetite disturbance—either eating too much or eating too little, difficulty concentrating, forgetfulness, and suicidal thoughts. If a person develops these symptoms he or she is certainly "running faster than he has strength."

President Brigham Young spoke about the need for balance. I often give this quote to workaholic Mormons. "Then let us seek to extend the present life, by observing every law of health, and by properly balancing labor, study, rest and recreation, and thus prepare for a better life" (2) People are often dumbfounded by this quote. They think there is no way they can find time in their busy schedules for daily recreation and relaxation with the demands of jobs, children, spouses, housework, school and even church. I can sympathize with these concerns since I work at two jobs and also have my calling as a bishop. However, I have somehow found time for regular relaxation, exercise and recreation.

A beautiful scripture in the Old Testament reminds us of the importance of balance.

"To every thing there is a season and a time to every purpose under the heaven:

"A time to be born, and a time to die; a time to plant, and a time to pluck up that which has been planted;

"A time to weep, and a time to laugh; a time to mourn, and a time to dance;

"A time to cast away stones, and a time to gather stones together; a time to embrace and a time to refrain from embracing.

Ecclesiastes 3:1,2,4,5

So many become totally engrossed in one aspect of their lives that they do it to the detriment of other important areas of their lives. Many husbands and fathers, for instance, are so obsessed with their jobs that they spend most of their time at work; and even when they do come home they are thinking and preparing for their jobs. Even when they are present at home they are really absent. Their minds are elsewhere.

To lead a balanced life includes the all-important ability to "compartmentalize." This means that when you are at work, you are at work. When you are at home and at play, you are at home and at play—you are fully present in all aspects of your life. We must concentrate on one thing at a time and have a rich variety to our lives. In the Gospel according to Luke, it is recorded that Martha was busy doing chores when she implored the Lord to get her sister, Mary, to help her. Mary was sitting at the Savior's feet learning from him. The Lord mildly chastised Martha for not recognizing what was most important and placing too much emphasis on work. (Luke 10:38-42)

Work is surely important; but rest, recreation, relaxation, enjoying the Spirit, and learning are just as important and deserve just as much of our attention. Truly successful people have learned to compartmentalize and lead well-balanced lives. The following are two such individuals who have learned balance despite their heavy work obligations:

It's unimaginable to think of the pressures that the President of the United States must be going through, especially since September 11. *Newsweek* reported recently how President George W. Bush copes with the tremendous stress of his job. He says his faith in God is tremendously important to him and he is "comforted" by his own prayers and the prayers of others. He takes a problem solving approach to life and does not spend a lot of time agonizing and theorizing. He is an avid runner and exercises for an hour every day. Despite the tremendous stress he reports he has never felt more confident and he does not live in fear. (3)

Elder Russell Nelson, before he was called as an apostle, worked in a very stressful profession as a heart surgeon. He, like President Bush, has also gained much of his strength from faith and prayer. He starts the day with an hour to himself praying, studying the scriptures and playing the organ. He and his family always look forward to holidays and vacations. In the summer he and his family water ski, swim, play tennis and horse back ride. In the winter he loves to ski. Elder Nelson has learned to not look back through the 'retrospectoscope' and agonize over the past and what he might have done differently. (4)

These are indeed examples of successful copers. Despite their extremely busy schedules they have learned to invest in themselves. Jesus Christ personifies selflessness and giving. Yet, even he spent time by himself recovering, resting and communing privately with God the Father. In Luke, it is recorded that Christ was laboring by preaching to throngs of people and blessing them. It then states that "he withdrew himself into the wilderness, and prayed." (Luke 5:16) Even he, the greatest of all, found it necessary to rest and recuperate and have time for solitude and privacy.

Clearly one of the most important reasons for taking care of our needs is for our mental and physical health. I would like to state another reason for taking care of our needs and spending time on ourselves by quoting Patricia Holland, wife of apostle Jeffrey Holland:

"The Lord often allows us to wallow in mindless

confusion before the teacher within us follows the path that lightens our way. Jeff and I were young married graduate students with two babies and heavy church assignments when President Harold B. Lee shared a prophet's counsel on order in chaos. An anxious physician worried that because of his profession and church responsibilities, he was neglecting his own son, asked President Lee how should I handle my time? What is most important in life? How do I do it all? President Lee replied: A man's first responsibility is to himself, then to his family, then to Church, realizing that we have responsibility to excel in our profession as well. He then stressed that a man must take care of his own health, both physically and emotionally, before he can be a blessing to others.

As a young woman I wrestled with this counsel, considering carefully how one taking care of herself first manages to lose herself for others. As the years passed, I saw how the truth in President Lee's counsel seemed to fit perfectly the order spoken of in the temple. The temple teaches priorities, it teaches order, it teaches growth, it teaches joy and fulfillment. Consider the following teachings from the temple (I have taken the words from the scriptures so that I will not inappropriately trifle with sacred things.)

In the fourth chapter of Abraham, the Gods plan the creation of the earth and all life thereon. In these plans (which take thirty-one versés to outline), the word or a form of the word *order* is used sixteen times. The Gods organize and give order to every living thing "And the Gods said: We will do everything that we have said, and organize them, and they will become very obedient" (Abraham 4:31) If we are to become like the Gods, we will begin with order. We will choose to obey the laws and principles of heaven which lead to order.

One of the first truths taught in the temple is that

"every living thing shall fill the measure of its creation" That is a powerful commandment. Consider it in light of President Lee's counsel. I must admit that when I first heard this directive I thought it meant only procreation: having issue, bearing offspring. I am sure that is the most important part of its meaning, but much of the temple ceremony is symbolic, so surely there are multiple meanings in that statement as well. How else does a woman fill the measure of her creation? How does she become all that her heavenly parents intend her to be? Growth, fulfillment, reaching, stretching, and developing our talents are part of the process of becoming like God, the ultimate "measure of our creation." (5)

Another important reason to take care of our needs and spend precious time on ourselves is to "fulfill the measure of our creation" We must find out what talents, gifts and abilities God has given us. How else can a person find out if he has a talent for music or art, for example, if he does not spend time on himself? Imagine if Johann Sebastian Bach had not taken time to develop his musical ability or if Michelangelo had not taken time for his artistic talent. The world would be missing some great masterpieces. Even so Heavenly Father has given us all talents. He wants and expects us to develop these talents. Developing and sharing these talents brings us great joy and happiness. I have fond memories of spending many, many hours in the privacy of my room practicing my trumpet and baritone. I also have great memories of playing in symphonic band and marching band and sharing this talent. Should we give up trying to develop our talents just because we reach adulthood and have many more responsibilities? I emphatically say "no." To give a positive example of this, I remember my wife developing her talent for playing the organ. She has played the piano since childhood but did not play the organ until she became an adult. She set this goal to develop this talent, took lessons and practiced many hours. Because of this she has gained much satisfaction and happiness from her new found talent and the ward has benefited as well.

The new core belief that I help clients to develop is "I must take care of my own needs first before giving to others." This sounds selfish to many and they recoil at the thought of making this their new belief. Nevertheless, this is what we need to obtain balance and happiness in our lives. To clarify this and perhaps to make this belief more palatable, let me clarify and differentiate between needs and wants. I regard safety and security, relaxation, recreation, rest, learning, to love and be loved as human needs as well the physical needs for food, water and air to sustain life. Wants, however, would include huge amounts of money, fame, "toys" like big screen TVs, DVDs, boats, snowmobiles, etc and going on expensive "flings" like cruises, vacations to Disneyland, expensive restaurants, etc. We must take care of our needs but its not always possible or even desirable to fill all our wants. Perhaps a little analogy will help explain this. I compare needs to fruits and vegetables and a steady healthy diet. However, wants are like chocolate and ice cream. Enjoying an occasional chocolate bar or ice cream cone is nice and will not hurt you. However, a steady diet of "wants" will make us fat and unhealthy in many ways. It will retard our emotional and spiritual progress as well.

Once a person decides to incorporate this new belief, his automatic thoughts will frequently appear to induce guilt. When a mother, for instance, takes some time to relax by reading a novel or enjoying a warm bath, she will have automatic thoughts most assuredly pop into her mind: "This is selfish." "This is wrong and sinful" However, this mother must counter with more positive, constructive thoughts like "I am not a selfish person. I am a generous, giving person but I deserve this time to myself. It will help me to be a more balanced, healthy person."

Like any core belief the best way to strengthen a new belief is to act on it. We act on this belief by taking some precious time for ourselves every day—preferably an hour a day to relax, develop a talent, read, exercise or something else. We must then protect this time. I have found it very essential in my life to get "spiritually grounded" every day. I do this by taking a few minutes a day reading the scriptures, praying, and meditating. I practice Dr. Herbert Benson's meditative technique called the Relaxation Response which only requires 10-20 minutes a day. (6) I also have found it very rejuvenating and advantageous to my health to exercise 4-5 days a week. In addition, I am always reading a fictional or non-fictional book.

To make this new belief possible is the all-important ability to say 'no' and establish strong boundaries. With practice this can be done in a very classy and non-offensive way e.g. "I'm so flattered that you asked me to participate on this committee but I just have too many other obligations right now. I'm going to have to decline but thanks for thinking of me and consider me again next year." This also means being able to say 'no' to our own family e.g. "Honey, mommy needs a little time for myself right now so please don't bother me during mommy's time I promise you I'll play with you later."

In closing, 2 Corinthians 9:7 states ". . . for God loveth a cheerful giver." There are so many people who routinely and frequently give but they do so resentfully. They are martyrs. This does not benefit any one and does not count as a blessing. Instead, when we do give we need to give joyfully and from the heart. We must fill up our own wells with water first then we will overflow with sparklingly pure, delicious water that others can freely partake.

CHAPTER 8

Sagging self-image

The problem of low self-esteem or a sagging self-image is a very common one. It's surprising who has this problem. I have known very intelligent, attractive, talented, moral people who, nevertheless, have low self-worth. Their core belief says "I am inferior to other people." or "I am a person of little or no worth" It is easy to see why children in abusive families would develop this belief. They are frequently called names like "stupid", "dumb", "fat", "ugly" and even worse epithets. Its also very difficult to feel good about one's self when he or she is regularly being hit, slapped, kicked or sexually abused.

When I talk about a client's past with him or her, its amazing how often a client can recall one single incident that occurred in childhood that had a devastating effect on his self-esteem. For example, I recall Jerry, age 35, who had problems with anger and depression. He recounted a time when he was ten years old and had just gotten a remote control airplane. He was flying his plane around the neighborhood and was attracting quite a few other kids who had come to watch. He was feeling quite proud of himself. However, he crashed his airplane and his father flew out of the house in a rage. He yelled at him and called him stupid in front of the other children and dragged him into the house. He was not hurt physically but he was totally humiliated. Although this incident happened twenty-five years ago he remembered it as clearly as if it had just happened yesterday and it still pained him greatly.

Another client by the name of Alice, age 62,

suffered from long-term depression. She told me she had struggled in school academically but when she was in the sixth grade she had a desire to play the violin. She told me her father was otherwise a good, loving father but when she approached him about playing the violin he angrily replied he couldn't afford to buy her a violin. He then thoughtlessly and cruelly added she was probably too stupid to play the violin anyway. That was crushing at her tender age to hear that burning criticism from this person she loved and respected. It left a deep scar that lasted for over forty years. These examples should impress on us parents how really fragile our children are and how one careless remark can tremendously wound a child's self-esteem.

This core belief can also develop in homes where there is no verbal abuse whatsoever and where the parents are very loving and caring. As a child enters school with some kind of obvious weakness, he or she is at risk. The other children often tease and harass the child unmercifully about this weakness. For example, perhaps the child is short and thin for his age. He or she may struggle academically because of a learning disability. Perhaps the child is from a poor home and is teased because he or she does not dress in fashionable clothes and is forced to wear hand-me-downs. Not all children with weaknesses or handicaps develop low self-worth but it is extremely common. This core belief about inferiority can literally last a life time and have a huge negative impact on a person's life. They are usually very vulnerable to depression. They often become very shy and reclusive and do not develop important social skills. It prevents them from taking risks and jumping at golden opportunities because they decide they will fail any way and they do not want to go through any further embarrassment or shame. These are just some of the potential negative side effects that come from having this belief.

It is difficult to overcome such a belief but certainly possible. I know that not only as a therapist but also as a bishop and a follower of Christ. I believe very firmly that through the atonement of Christ we can all let go of the past and change. To begin this process, these clients need to be reminded of their great intrinsic worth. I like to quote them D&C 18:10 "Remember the worth of souls is great in the sight of God" and Psalms 8: 4,5: "What is man, that thou art mindful of him. For thou hast made him a little lower than the angels, and hast crowned him with glory and honor" Regular scripture study can be very elevating and uplifting and reminds us how very special we are in God's eyes. We are literally His children and have the potential to be as He is.

A very common cognitive error that depressed people do is called selective attention or mental filter. When they look back at their lives all they can see is the failures and negative events. This confirms their belief that they are inferior and of little worth. Its as if they are wearing blinders that only allow them to see the negative. As a brief example of this, I remember Susan, age 38, who was a very beautiful, intelligent, kind woman who had depression and did selective attention often. She told me she got a letter from her sister-in-law and the letter was generally positive and full of compliments and praise. However, the sister-in-law included one minor criticism. For several days Susan obsessed about this criticism and thought that her sister-in-law saw her as worthless and no good. She completely ignored the positive part of the letter which comprised of most of the letter.

Recently I attended a conference where Dr. Donald Meichenbaum was one of the main speakers. He is renowned cognitive-behavioral therapist. He said it is necessary to talk to clients about their past and all the negative things that have happened in their lives, which is usually considerable. It often includes abuse of every kind, deaths of loved ones, and other traumatic events. They have often lived very tragic lives full of suffering and pain. However, after gathering that history it is important to go back and do an "in spite of" time line with them. He says in every person's life there are accomplishments, achievements and other positive events that have been totally forgotten because of selective attention. He compares this "in spite of" time line to Paul Harvey's radio commentary "the rest of the story" (1) In every person's life there is a "rest of the story" that confirms this person's worth and strengths but it is often not focused on or remembered.

As an analogy, I read a newspaper article about a year ago that I found fascinating about the Mbuji-Mayi community in the Congo. In this land ravaged by civil war, the people live in poverty and dwell in mud huts with no running water or paved streets. Yet, this community is known for its diamonds. Diamonds are plentiful in this community and they used to be so common that members of the community would adorn the walls of their mud huts with them. Now boys as young as eight years old go to the mines and dig through the mud and dirt to find unpolished diamonds. Sometimes after a good rainfall diamonds can be seen in the dirt and mud. (2) To me this community with its valuable gems are symbolic of our minds. Often when we look back on our lives all we remember is the negative events, the failures and the disappointments. Yet just under the mud and dirt of our consciousness diamonds can be found. With the help of a therapist we remember the spelling contest we won in the third grade. We remember making the basketball team in junior high. We may remember helping another student in elementary school who was ignored and mistreated. These diamonds exist in everyone's lives but are not focused on and are usually forgotten or ignored.

The gospel teaches similar concepts. The Lord blesses every body with some diamonds in the form of talents and strengths. As the old saying goes: "God didn't create no junk" I am reminded of the parable of the talents in Matthew 25: 14-30. The Lord gave one of his servants five talents, another servant two talents and another servant only one talent. The servant who had five talents doubled his talents through work and industry as did the servant who had two talents. However, the servant who only had one talent was ashamed and buried his talent in the ground. The Lord was very pleased with his two servants who had doubled their talents but he was not pleased with the servant who hid his talent and did not use it. He rebuked that unprofitable servant and cast him out. So it is with all of us. Some people have more talents and strengths than others but the Lord has given us all at least one talent that we can succeed with. We all have the potential of making our lives successful. We just need to believe in ourselves and make the best of what we have been given and not dwell upon what we do not have.

A great example of this is the LDS Olympic athlete Rulon Gardner. He grew up in a large family on a diary farm in Wyoming. As a child he was not the picture of a highly gifted, popular child. He struggled academically and had learning disabilities. He also weighed 125 lb. in the fourth grade. He was teased by other children and called "fatso". He was blessed, however, with two talents and those were his strong work ethic and his athletic ability. He did go on to become a state champion in wrestling in high school in Wyoming. He also went on to become a champion at

Ricks College and later an All-American at the University of Nebraska. He also made the Olympic team. He then had the ultimate test in his sport of Greco-Roman wrestling when he faced the Russian, Alexander Karelin in the 2000 Olympics in Sydney, Australia. Karelin had never lost and he was highly favored over Rulon. In one of the greatest upsets in the history of the Olympics, what Sports Illustrated called the "miracle on the mat", Rulon beat Karelin in a 1-0 decision (3) One can imagine how easy it would have been for Rulon to give into discouragement and depression when he was a child. He could have easily developed a core belief that he was inferior and a failure. However, with the help of God and good parents he did develop what talents the Lord had given him and became very successful as an Olympic champion. Of his childhood, Rulon said it was "kind of tough" because of the teasing but "I used those insults as motivation" (4)

The new core belief I attempt to instill in my clients is "I have been blessed with talents and abilities. I am equal to others. I am or can be successful with my God given abilities and talents" By equal I emphasize that means he or she is equal to anybody and that literally means anybody. I am equal to President George W. Bush, Bill Gates, or even President Gordon B. Hinckley. God does not value one of his children more than another and neither should we think that we have less value or worth than any one else. We all need to believe that we have infinite worth and are successful.

For many clients with sagging self-image this is a very hard core belief to accept. Their whole lives they have literally spent thinking of themselves as inferior. Even if they want to it is extremely difficult to see themselves in any other way. To paraphrase Alma 32, I counsel my clients that even if you can only exercise a particle of faith or a desire to believe this new belief then let it work in you. Pretend it is a seed and plant it in your heart. If you will nourish the seed with diligence and patience it will begin to sprout and take root. The new core belief will begin to swell within your breast and you will begin to recognize it is a good seed and it will become delicious to you.

There are a number of ways a person can nourish this belief. It does require diligence, patience, faith and persistent effort. A common technique I use with many clients involves imagery. I have clients close their eyes and recall a time when they felt depressed and had low self-confidence. I then ask them to imagine the same situation but this time imagine that they have the new belief. I have them imagine how they would think differently and how they would behave differently according to their new belief. This technique derives from the principle that if I can imagine it then I can do it and is a powerful way to reinforce the new core belief

Another way to strengthen a new belief requires that we gather evidence for the new core belief daily. In a homework assignment I have used from Greenburger & Padesky (5), clients gather evidence to support their new belief by writing down three things daily in a journal or log that confirm their new belief. Even if it seems trivial, I encourage them to write it down. It may be something as simple as a compliment from a co-worker or a friend or a good feeling after completing a project. This requires a change in focus. Instead of dwelling and focusing on our shortcomings and failures this exercise requires us to focus on our strengths and successes. We all have successes daily even though they may be small. Some days we have huge successes. A client desiring this new belief should also pray and ask Heavenly Father to strengthen the new belief.

I remember one of my clients, Cathy, a sweet,

cute 24-year old returned missionary who suffered from low self-esteem and depression for most of her life. She is a good example of what I have been discussing in this chapter. Even though she had many talents and strengths she did not focus on them and instead focused only on her mistakes and weaknesses. This blond, blue-eyed beauty grew up in a home with a cold, domineering mother and a withdrawn, distant father. As a result, she developed a core belief that she was inferior to others and that belief stayed with her even though she was successful in many aspects of her life. She was successful academically and even went on to obtain a college degree. She was talented musically as a pianist and singer and had given several, excellent performances in her life. She completed a successful mission. She also possessed many lovely personality traits such as being caring and compassionate. Like all of us, she too had her weaknesses and had made some mistakes. Craving attention from men to desperately boost her sagging self-esteem, she engaged in some immorality. She repented fully of these transgressions and yet she could not forgive herself. Those mistakes confirmed her belief that she was inferior.

I assisted her in developing a new belief that she was equal to others and was talented and successful. I asked her to do the exercise of logging three positive accomplishments or strengths every day to confirm her new belief. She responded by saying: "Isn't this being boastful and proud" I strongly replied "no"! I explained there is a huge difference between being proud and believing in oneself. People who are proud and boastful usually have underlying insecurity and low self-esteem that they are vainly trying to cover up. Being proud, boastful, or narcissistic is one of Carl Jung's "masks" or "false selves" that I referred to in chapter three. It is not our authentic selves. People who believe in themselves, on the other hand, have a quiet self-confidence and go about their business without any fanfare or self-aggrandizement. They are usually very successful but at the same time remain humble. They are teachable and welcome feedback from others whether it be good or negative. They continually acknowledge God's hand in all things and give him thanks for their accomplishments and gifts.

Cathy did what I asked her to do. She very gradually started to believe her new belief about her self. It was slow in the beginning but after a while her new belief began to take root. She came into her own and became happier than she had ever been. At last report, Cathy had married in the temple to a fine man and she was supremely happy.

As clients start to gather evidence for their new belief and honestly begin to believe the new core belief, other people begin to take notice. It may start out slowly at first but after a while many clients, like Cathy, actually blossom and are transformed. They become very happy and joyful. They begin to try new things and take risks. They set up goals and accomplish them. This is very gratifying to a therapist. Of course, I strongly believe Jesus Christ is helping them in this process and the angels in heaven are cheering them on. There is much joy in heaven over these individuals who are actually believing in themselves for the first time and loving themselves. Their names are written on the marquees in heaven.

In closing I would like to quote Nelson Mandela. I found this quote to be very inspiring and appropriate.

"Our deepest fear is not that we are inadequate. Our deepest fear is that we powerful beyond measure.

It is our light not our darkness that most frightens us.

We ask ourselves, who am I to be brilliant, gorgeous, talented and fabulous?

Actually, who are you not to be?

You are a child of God. Your playing small doesn't serve the world.

There's nothing enlightened about shrinking so that other people won't feel insecure around you.

We were born to make manifest the glory of God that is within us.

It's not just in some of us; it's in everyone.

And as we let our own light shine, we unconsciously give other people permission to do the same.

As we are liberated from our own fear, our presence automatically liberates others." (6)

I have discussed the **PENS** core beliefs in these last four chapters. Thus far, I have emphasized how to overcome depression by changing these key core beliefs. Now I would like to turn my attention to three more common emotional problems in the Church, as well as among many good and honorable people and that is anxiety, anger and addictions.

CHAPTER 9

Anxiety

Depression is never beneficial or appropriate but anxiety is a different story. Some anxiety is appropriate and even beneficial. It can, for instance, warn us of danger and mobilize us for action. Fear and anxiety can even be fun. How many people enjoy going to a scary movie or riding a thrill ride at an amusement park? Most of us do enjoy some fear and anxiety to a certain degree. However, anxiety can become so disabling and chronic that it becomes a disorder. Let us discuss panic as an example. Most of us have experienced panic at some time. Most members of the Church, for instance, can relate to the panic many have experienced before giving a talk. It is very common to experience sweating, trembling, heavy breathing and a racing pulse up to 140 beats per minute just prior to and while giving a talk. Having these panicky feelings is not any cause for concern and is very common.

Certain people, however, become overly concerned about their panic. They develop a "fear of the fear." This leads to avoidance of the fear and subsequently the development of a phobia. Some, for instance, develop a public speaking phobia and go to great lengths to avoid speaking in public. Sometimes even at the peril of losing their jobs or getting a demotion he or she will avoid speaking in front of a group. Another person may have a close call in an automobile and feel shaken. Rather than "getting back on the horse" he will stop driving and develop a driving phobia. When a person avoids a fear it reinforces and strengthens the fear. The fear starts to take over.

Sometimes the phobia stays confined to a certain situation but other times the fear may generalize to other situations and becomes "agoraphobia." The unfortunate sufferers of this disorder can literally become house bound by their fears.

People with phobias seem to have a core belief that says: "My fear will continue to escalate until I go crazy, lose control or die" They often imagine something outlandish happening such as severely embarrassing themselves or becoming psychotic during their panic. They also often fear having a heart attack or dying. This is almost never the case but to these sufferers it seems like a very real possibility. These imaginings only strengthen the phobia and strengthen the desire to escape.

Phobias can cause any where from mild impairment to severe impairment. It takes a great deal of courage and determination to overcome a phobia. Paul said: "God hath not given us the spirit of fear; but of power, and of love, and of a sound mind." (2 Timothy 1:7) It takes all of these attributes of power, strength, love of God and self and a sound, rational mind to over come a phobia.

Dr. Clair Weekes, an Australian psychiatrist, gave a formula for overcoming fear and panic. In order to overcome a phobia, a person needs to: *face, accept, float and let time pass.* (1) By "facing a fear" she means not running away from the fear and stopping the avoidance behavior. In fact, a person actually needs to seek out situations that trigger the fear in order to practice and learn to cope with the fear. A person with a fear of heights, for instance, may need to deliberately go into tall buildings in order to overcome this fear. "Accepting the fear" means that the phobic person needs to accept and even expect the fear to arise. By expecting and accepting the fear, it robs the fear of its power. When a person expects to become panicky in a certain situation then when it does come it is almost never as bad as the person imagined it would be. It is ironic but one of the most powerful ways of coping with a fear is by accepting and expecting it to come.

During this process it is important to stay positive in one's thoughts. You need to encourage yourself with thoughts such as: "I can handle this", "I'm still in control. I just need to concentrate on what I need to do" "The fear will certainly pass" "I'm doing really well" Conversely, if one has negative, catastrophic thoughts, such as: "I'm having a heart attack;" "I'm going crazy;" "I'm losing control;" "I'm dying;" then that is like dumping gasoline on a fire. These negative thoughts will certainly amplify those fears and make it much worse. A phobic person can learn to "talk himself down" with positive thoughts when he is having fear and this helps a great deal to cope with the fear.

The concept of "floating a fear" is more difficult concept to explain. When the fear comes, as it certainly will, Dr. Weekes says you can float the fear. She says you can imagine the fear as a river of water and just let it flow through your body. The fear will not harm you physically and you need to let it flow through your nerve cells. You do not make any attempt to impede it or obstruct it. You just let it float freely through your nervous system. In some ways, it is healthy to experience this fear as it cleanses you of your insecurities. Ultimately it strengthens you to face and experience your fears and it builds character. It is a tremendous act of courage to confront these fears. It makes us stronger and healthier people once we have overcome the fear. This is in direct contrast to the core belief that says our panic and fear is dangerous and we must avoid it at all costs.

Debbie Ford's words are especially appropriate

here and are similar to the concept of floating. She says that anything we *resist persists.* This is certainly true of phobias. Avoiding and resisting the fear only reinforces the fear and assures that it will continue.. She says: "Our initial response is always to resist any perceived threat. Yet it is only when we breath deep, relax, and lean into the experience that we stand strong and gain access to all our power and strength" (2)

By "let time pass", Dr. Weekes says that panics do not usually last longer than ten minutes. You just wait it out and the fear will eventually subside - especially if you keep focused on the task at hand and stay positive. As you are confronting your fear, you stay grounded in the present and not imagine what might or could happen. After a short time, the panic runs its course and the river of fear runs dry.

I found this poem several years ago that summarizes well how to confront our fears:

Today, I let the bull pass
As the matador does not stand
there to be gored,
I gracefully step aside.
and let
all negative forces
go by me.
I remain
centered and balanced,
not resisting
but
flexible..
As I see the negative
attitude, habit, or person
confronting me,
I nimbly turn,
as does the matador,

and the destructive energy
finds no target.
                              -Author Unknown

A matador does not run away from the bull but bravely faces the bull. He lets it come and skillfully lets it pass. He stays expertly balanced and focused in the present and concentrates on the task at hand. He confronts the bull over and over again until he has conquered the bull and it no longer poses a threat.

I have emphasized to this point accepting and confronting our fears. However, as you are confronting your fears there are some other things you can do to help you cope. The first is correct breathing, or "belly breathing". Many people when they become fearful breath too fast and take short, shallow breaths from their chests. This may lead to hyperventilation. Abdominal or belly breathing means deliberately slowing your breathing and breathing deep into your abdomen. As you inhale for five seconds, your stomach should expand. While you exhale to the same count of five your belly deflates. Taking 8-10 deep breaths in a frightening situation can greatly help you to feel better and more in control.

Another very common tactic for overcoming fears is called "exposure therapy' and was developed by behavioral therapists. This means that you systematically and gradually expose yourself to the feared situation. You do not try to face it all at once. You give yourself doses of fear. You construct a "fear hierarchy" and confront the least fearful aspect of the phobia first until you have over come this fear and have gained confidence. You are then ready to move up the ladder and tackle the more difficult aspect of your fear. I can illustrate this with an example. Billy, age 10, was a former client of mine. He was savagely bitten by a dog and he developed a phobia of dogs. He would even avoid puppies and friendly dogs. This fear affected his walk to school in the morning and he was terrified to have to pass by a dog even though the dog was friendly. I constructed a fear hierarchy with him. First, he started by just looking at pictures of dogs. He then moved on to being within twenty feet of a friendly puppy. He then came within ten feet of the puppy. Gradually, he was able to stand next to the puppy. All this time, his parents were encouraging and rewarding him for confronting his fear. Very gradually he was able to pet the puppy. Eventually he overcame the fear altogether. Of course, it is always a good idea to avoid vicious, dangerous dogs but Billy overcame his phobia altogether and it no longer negatively impacts his life.

Another great fear reducer is prayer. The scriptures are full of wonderfully inspiring stories where people prayed for strength in perilous times and the Lord comforted, aided and abetted his people. The righteous Nephites, for example, were often confronted with some very frightening situations. However, they prayed mightily and put their trust in the Lord and they were comforted, strengthened, and almost invariably blessed with victory. In chapter four of 3 Nephi, for instance, the Gadianton robbers had amassed a great army to battle the Nephites. The Gadiation robbers had dyed themselves with blood and shorn their heads to appear as intimidating as possible. When the Nephites saw the army of Gadianton robbers they fell to the earth. The robbers rejoiced because they mistakenly thought the Nephites had fallen down in fear. However, the Nephites had fallen to their knees in prayer. It states that "the Nephites did not fear them; but they did fear their God and did supplicate him for protection . . . they were prepared to meet them; yea, in the strength of the Lord they did meet them." (v. 10) The Nephites went on to defeat the robbers with a great slaughter. I can testify myself that prayer has greatly comforted and strengthened me in times of need and apprehension.

I must tell you about my own struggle with fear and panic. As a young man I developed a public speaking phobia. I had the familiar symptoms of panic i.e. trembling, sweating, heart palpitations, etc.; whenever I gave a speech or talk. Unfortunately, instead of accepting these symptoms as normal I started to avoid public speaking. This only reinforced the fear. There was a period in my life when I would not give talks and speeches. God certainly knows our weaknesses and fears and He gives us opportunities to over come these fears. I remember clearly the day when I was confronted with my most dreaded fear. I was called to be a high councilman! This was the most frightening call I could have possibly received! It was indeed sink or swim time and even though I was terrified, I decided it was time I confront and over come this fear.

I used the techniques I have described in this chapter to over come this fear. I certainly prayed to the Lord in mighty, heartfelt prayer. There were some other techniques that I utilized that were very helpful to me. One technique is called "covert rehearsal". There is much power in our imagination and in this technique one utilizes the power of imagination. Oftentimes our imaginations work against us and we imagine the very worst. This is called "catastrophizing" as mentioned earlier in this chapter. Our bodies respond to the catastrophic imaginings by sweating, rapid breathing, racing heart, etc. In this technique you imagine being in a very idyllic scene in nature. You imagine this scene as clearly and vividly as you can. After relaxing yourself by imagining this peaceful situation, you then imagine being in the feared situation. However, instead of imagining yourself going psychotic or falling apart you imagine yourself coping and doing well. I would imagine myself being confident and giving a good talk. If you become too tense or anxious while imaging the feared situation then you can go back into your idyllic "safe place" in nature and relax. You are then ready to give it another try and imagine being back in the feared situation. In this way, you can desensitize yourself somewhat to the fearful situation in real life.

Another technique is called distraction. While in the throes of anxiety a person can distract himself temporarily and get his mind off of how anxious he is. The anxiety subsequently goes down—at least momentarily. While waiting to stand up to give my speech, I would often distract myself. I would count down by sevens from 100 silently to myself. This requires some concentration and would get my mind off how anxious I was feeling. I would also flip open my scriptures or a hymnbook and start reading. Some people recite a favorite song or hymn when afraid. This distraction helped me to manage my fear.

Finally, another method for overcoming fear that I utilized is called "flooding" by behavioral therapists. Instead of working up to the most fearful situation in gradated steps, this method involves exposing yourself to your most dreaded fear all at once. The theory behind this concept is that by facing your most severe fear and not running away, the fear eventually subsides and you then extinguish the fear. Usually it takes several trials for the fear to completely go away. I was certainly flooding myself with fear by accepting this call to be a high councilor. Just before getting up to give my talk, I would actually dare myself to get panicky. I would say to myself. "If I am going to have a panic attack then I want to have a whopper! Bring it on!" By facing and accepting my fear like this it invariably was never that bad. I never did go crazy or severely embarrass myself like I thought I would.

I calculated that I gave 36 talks as a high councilor. I can honestly say now that I enjoy giving talks and speeches and actually seek out opportunities to speak. I still get somewhat nervous but not nearly as bad as I used to. I thank the Lord that I had the courage to accept this challenge and not "shrink and shun the fight."

I will summarize how to overcome panic and phobia:

1. Make a determination to face the fear and accept and expect the fear to rise as you confront it. At the same time realizing the fear cannot hurt you.

2. Use positive self-talk and prayer while confronting the fear and give yourself pep talks and encouragement while you successfully "talk down" the fear. The Lord can and often comforts and strengthens as you ask for his help.

3. Watch your breathing and practice abdominal breathing

4. Construct a fear hierarchy and practice over and over again facing the fear until you have successfully overcome the phobia and it no longer scares you or negatively affects your life.

5. Find what technique works for you whether it be covert rehearsal, distraction, exposure therapy or flooding. Take advantage of opportunities God gives to you to over come your fears.

Worry

Many people do not experience panics but

nevertheless their lives are filled with worry. This can develop into a mental disorder called Generalized Anxiety Disorder. Some worry is normal but some people worry excessively about almost everything. The worry can precipitate physical symptoms like muscle tension and pain, difficulty falling asleep, irritability, and being easily startled. Some of this excessive worry could very well be genetic and biological. However, many people grow up in unsettled, frightening homes and they develop a core belief that says: "The worst is bound to happen. I must be on my guard all the time and be prepared for the worst" Like phobic people, they doubt their ability to successfully cope with their problems and have low confidence in themselves. Like many people who suffer from depression, they figure it is their lot in life to suffer and they never seek treatment. They often commit a cognitive error called "catastro-phizing" as mentioned earlier. These people are like Chicken Little who was hit on the head by a falling acorn and ran about crying "the sky is falling". They invariably imagine the worst possible scenario. I like this quote by Montaigne who recognized this tendency in himself when he said: "My life has been full of terrible misfortunes- Most of which never happened" We all know these types of people and may even be guilty of catastrophizing ourselves sometimes.

In overcoming worry, I have developed a tech-nique called throwing doubt on your doubt. This requires you to think as rationally and clearly as you can. Worry usually involves some thing or event that has yet to occur. Many of the events that you worry about are very improbable. Ask yourself these questions: "How likely is it that this feared event will occur?" "Am I more likely to be hit by a bolt of lightening or be hit by a train than experience this frightening event?" "Has anything remotely resembling this ever occurred to me before?" When you ask your-self such questions you can often see how very unlikely and even preposterous your worries are and you can dismiss them.

For more realistic worries, Dr. Ned Hallowell, a prominent psychiatrist, laid out five steps for managing worry.

1. Never worry alone. Share your worries with others and get their opinion.

2. Get the facts. Much worry is due to not having enough facts and you need to gather as much information and facts as possible about the problem you are worrying about.

3. Develop a plan. Making up a plan of action can be tremendously helpful in alleviating your worries. It mobilizes you for action and helps you reasonably do what you can. You then put the rest in the Lord's hands.

4. Take care of yourself physically. This means getting enough sleep, eating properly, exercising and taking good care of yourself.

5. Let go of the worry. He said this is the most difficult step of all but you need to do what you can to solve your problem and tell yourself you have done everything you can possibly do and let go of the worry. This may very well require God's help. (3)

I have taught clients some very helpful relaxation techniques that do work. These include meditation, guided imagery, and as mentioned earlier deep breathing. However, the greatest source of relaxation is the Holy Ghost. As Christ said: "Peace I leave with you, my peace give I unto you; not as the world giveth, give I unto you. Let not your heart be troubled neither let it be afraid." As mentioned in an earlier chapter, it is so important to take a few minutes each day to pray, ponder and read the scriptures. This can be comforting and can settle your nerves.

A new core belief that sufferers of generalized anxiety must develop goes very much like a scripture from the New Testament: "And we know that all things work together for good to them that love God." (Romans 8:28) Another scripture from Paul is appropriate here: "There is no temptation taken you but such as is common to man; but God is faithful, who will not suffer you to be tempted above that ye are able; but will with the temptation also make a way to escape, that ye be able to bear it." (1 Cor 10:13) This is where you must develop a deep and abiding trust and faith in your Heavenly Father. He will protect you and be with you at all times. Life generally works out for the best as long as you are earnestly attempting to keep the command-ments and love God. Also, you must believe that God is faithful and He will always be there to comfort you and buoy you up when you go through your trials and challenges. You can accomplish anything and you can successfully cope with any problem as long as God is with you. You can be transformed from a nervous, jittery, worried well to a calm, peaceful person who is full of love and hope through Jesus Christ.

CHAPTER 10

Anger

Anger is a misunderstood emotion. Many people think it is a sin to even feel the emotion of anger. I am not of that opinion. Anger is a normal human emotion and indicates that our boundaries have been violated in some way. Sometimes anger can even be beneficial. Many places in the scriptures it indicates that the prophets and even the Lord himself felt righteous anger. One of my favorite heroes in the *Book of Mormon* is Captain Moroni. This great Nephite military leader was described by Mormon as a "strong and mighty man". He was also a very righteous and faithful man. Mormon said of Moroni that if all men were like Moroni then "the very powers of hell would have been shaken forever" (Alma 48:17) Yet in the *Book of Mormon* it indicates Moroni was often angry. The wickedness of the Lamanites, the traitors Amlickiah and his brother, Ammoron, and even his own people at times angered Moroni. For instance, it states: "And now Moroni was angry because of the stubbornness of the Lamanites." (Alma 44:17) But this anger motivated him to defeat the enemies of the nation and of God.

In therapy, feeling anger can be beneficial and even therapeutic. For instance, when dealing with depressed clients who have been victimized their whole lives, I sometimes encourage them to get in touch with their anger. It can be a positive sign when a victim of sexual abuse, for example, gets in touch with the anger she has repressed. Instead of pointing her anger inward toward herself and blaming herself, she is encouraged to point the anger outward toward those who deserve the anger—such as the perpetrator. Of course, violence and aggressive acts are not encouraged but there are appropriate, safe ways of expressing repressed anger. One such way is letter writing, which letter a victim may or may not send to the perpetrator.

The Lord commands all of us to forgive and so we should. In the Sermon on the Mount, the Lord says "Love your enemies, bless them that curse you, do good to them that hate you and pray for them which despitefully use you and persecute you" (Matt 5:44) Forgiveness is also the goal in therapy. However, forgiveness is a process and often requires extensive time for many people to achieve. Many have to be given the opportunity to feel the anger first before they can let it go and forgive. A good therapist can help a victim work through their anger and eventually reach this stage of complete forgiveness.

At times anger can be sinful. When anger is not controlled or justified, for example, that constitutes sin. President Gordon B. Hinckley has cautioned us about *uncontrolled anger* and he counsels us to *bridle our anger* and *school our feelings. (1)* This implies that it is inevitable that we all feel anger some times. We should seek to promote peace and love in our hearts but there will be times when we will feel anger. We need to control these feelings.

Some people suffer from chronic anger. They are angry several times a day and seem to get angry at the drop of a hat. This is not a healthy state to be in either mentally or physically. Chronically angry people, for instance, have a higher rate of heart attacks. (2) Their anger alienates people and sometimes injures others. Even though their anger may give them a sense of power they make a lot of enemies and sooner or later someone usually gets even with them.

Victims of child abuse sometimes develop

chronic anger. Instead of developing low self-worth and becoming passive and depressed, they go on the offensive and acquire a huge "chip on their shoulder" They develop a core belief that says: "The world is out to get me and I must be prepared to fight all the time." The cognitive error they commit is called "misattribution" They often attribute malevolent motives where there is none. They take offense where no offense was intended. They are referred to in the scriptures as those who are "easily provoked."

I will illustrate this with an example. Jack was a 31-year old man with a serious anger problem. Jack became angry several times a day. He would usually get angry just driving home from work if someone, for example, inadvertently cut in front of him and forced him to slow down. He developed "road rage" before it was even popular. He often exploded at his wife and children. Although he would refrain from becoming physically violent with his family, he would frequently yell and get verbally abusive. Sometimes he would throw things and break things when angry. Jack grew up in a home with six older brothers. He was also the "runt" of the family. He was teased and harassed unmercifully by his older brothers. He developed a huge chip on his shoulder. He very much had a core belief that the world was out to get him and he must fight back. In some ways this benefited him- on the football field, for instance. However, in most ways this did not benefit him. He had numerous conflicts with his boss and co-workers. His wife was on the verge of divorcing him when I started therapy with him. Utilizing cognitive therapy and a process I will describe in this chapter. I was able to help Jack let go of his chronic anger and find peace.

Even some "normal" people are sometimes guilty of misattribution. I am normally a calm person who seldom gets angry. But I have at times been guilty of misattribution. I have a love-hate relationship with my dog. I did not want a dog to begin with but my children talked me into it. He was an adorable puppy but, alas, puppies do grow up and adult dogs are much less interesting and cute. My dog, Cisco, is actually quite a good dog most of the time. He is very loving and well-behaved most of the time. However, sometimes I really become angry at him. The behavior that angers me the most is his barking. It seems like he barks for any reason - like a leaf falling off a tree. However, I have been chiding myself for getting so angry at him. I seem to interpret his barking as a deliberate attempt on his part to bother me and disobey me. However, dogs are naturally territorial and every dog alive barks when someone or something, like a cat, invades its territory. I still do not like his barking, but I have been trying to change my negative self-talk and not take it so personally when he barks.

Like described in earlier chapters, in order to change we must interrupt the automatic thoughts. The best way to do this with angry people is to take "time outs". Many people attempt to take time outs but they do not do it effectively. They take time outs, for example, after the damage has been done and hurtful things have already been said or done. Or a husband may storm off and leave but he leaves for hours and his wife is left at home frantically worrying whether he is ever coming home or if he is hurt. In order for a time out to be effective all participants must agree ahead of time on the terms of the time out. A time frame should be put on the time out. I usually recommend that a time out be at least twenty minutes but not longer than two hours. He or she must call for a time out as soon as he or she feels anger. In order to do this a person must be aware of his anger cues, which may include tense muscles, clenched teeth, feeling hot, sweating, etc. When a person calls for a time out the other person must agree ahead of time to let the person go without any protest and without firing any last moment volleys as he is exiting the room

A definite cue that indicates that a time out is necessary is when either person's voice is rising and he or she begins yelling. Some people feel yelling is appropriate when feeling anger but I do not. My father, who is now deceased, was a terrific yeller. He could lift the roof off the house with his yelling. Yelling can be very frightening, as I was frightened by my father's yelling. Yelling usually escalates into a fight or argument. It is very seldom productive and causes resentment, defensiveness, and fear. As David O. McKay said: "There should be no yelling in the home unless there is a fire"

During the time out is an excellent opportunity to examine your thoughts and modify your thinking by taking different perspectives. Looking at the conflict as a problem to be resolved rather than taking it personally as an offense is very helpful in reducing anger. It is very beneficial to consider the other person's point of view. Even though you may not agree with the other person's opinion, it is important to try to understand her view of things if this conflict is to be resolved peacefully and fairly. Doing a physical cool down like walking, running, exercising during the time out is also very beneficial in de-escalating the anger. President Brigham Young talked about his own struggle with his anger and described something very similar to time outs.

"Many men will say they have a violent temper, and try to excuse themselves for actions of which they are ashamed. I will say, there is not a man in this house who has a more indomitable and unyielding temper than myself. But there is not a man in the world who cannot overcome his passion, if he will struggle earnestly to do so. If you find passion coming on you, go off to some place where you cannot be heard; let none of your family see you or hear you, while it is upon you, but struggle till it leaves you; and pray for strength to overcome. When my feelings are aroused by the ill-doings of others, I hold them as I would a wild horse, and I gain the victory. Some think and say that it makes them feel better when they are mad, as they call it, to give vent to their madness in abusive and unbecoming language. This, however, is a mistake. Instead of it making you feel better you give credit to a falsehood.— You should succeed in bringing your tongues into subjection." (3)

Jesus gave some guidelines for dealing with conflict. He said: "Therefore if thou bringest thy gift to the alter, and there rememberest that thy brother has ought against thee; Leave there thy gift before the alter, and go thy way; first be reconciled to thy brother, and then come and offer thy gift." (Matt 5:23, 24) "Moreover if thy brother shall trespass against thee, go and tell him his fault between thee and him alone; if he shall hear thee, thou hast gained a brother" (Matt 18: 15)

After an offended person has taken his time out he or she can approach the other person involved and arrange a time to discuss the problem. Both parties should agree to talk at a time when they are feeling calm and will not be interrupted. They each express how they feel in a non-blaming and non-offensive way. It is important that while one person is talking the other person listens attentively. Without interrupting, the listener makes a sincere attempt to understand the problem from the other person's point of view. It will then be his turn to speak and express his feelings. They then brainstorm together on how to solve the problem. They decide on a plan of action they both feel good about. This is what Stephen Covey calls "Win-Win" problem solving as opposed to "Win-Lose" problem solving where there is a winner and loser. In this problem solving process both parties can be winners. (4)

The gospel can help angry people develop a new core belief. The gospel encourages us to have love in our hearts toward all men, as Christ loves us. A new core belief could in effect say: "We are all brothers and sisters. I will assume the best in others. Every person I meet is a potential friend" In regard to over coming misattribution, a person could develop a belief such as "Problems and conflicts are inevitable and normal between friends and I will not take offense when differences arise. I will look for a solution or forgive and forget"

To strengthen this belief one should pray for charity. "Charity suffereth long, and is kind, and envieth not, and is not puffed up, seeketh not her own, is not easily provoked, thinketh no evil, and rejoiceth not in iniquity but rejoiceth in the truth, bearth all things, believeth all things, hopeth all things, endureth all things. Wherefore, my beloved brethern, if ye have not charity, ye are nothing, for charity never faileth. Wherefore cleave unto charity, which is the greatest of all." (Moroni 7:45-46)

As an example of a person who was able to overcome anger through Christ-like love and charity is Paul. Paul is a 50 year old, Vietnam Veteran who I have been counseling with for several years. It is not often that I am intimidated by a client but Paul is a big, very strong man who resembles a grizzly bear and when I first started counseling with Paul I was very intimidated. He had the disposition of a grizzly bear also and was very angry and defensive. When I first talked to Paul he told me how he could easily throw me through the wall. He delighted in telling me all the ways he could easily kill anybody he desired by snapping their neck or by some other deadly and efficient way. I looked for all the ways I could to possibly get out of counseling with Paul but to no avail. Another counselor consulted with me about Paul and together we came up with the idea to have Paul start attending Alcoholics Anonymous, as he is a former alcoholic. A.A. is a spiritual organization and A.A. awakened something in Paul that had been asleep for many years and that was his soul. He started to remember the teachings of Christ from Catholicism that he had been taught as a child. Paul began to pray, read the *Bible*, attend church and practice his faith. Paul has gone through an amazing transformation and now Paul and I have become very close friends. We often talk about our mutual faith in Christ. He has become much kinder and gentler so that he now resembles more a huge teddy bear than a grizzly bear. It's remarkable that I could become so close to someone I used to so greatly fear. His core beliefs have changed also and instead of looking at others as potential enemies, he now sees others as potential brothers and sisters in Christ. Even though Paul is not a member of our faith, he is a prime example of how the gospel of Christ, in conjunction with therapy, can lead to a change of beliefs and a change of heart

Being in my calling as bishop has greatly increased charity in my own life and dispelled any anger or resentment I had. During sacrament and fast and testimony meeting, as I look out on the congregation, my heart is full and I can honestly say I love all of those who are present. Callings can do that. We love those whom we serve. Anger is quickly banished and the peace of the Holy Ghost fills our soul

CHAPTER 11

Addictions

I originally started my career as an alcohol and drug counselor. I have discovered that in no area does professional treatment and spirituality agree more than in the treatment of addictions. This is largely due to the popularity and success of Alcoholics Anonymous. I have since discovered in my career that many people struggle with addictions. In fact, I would go even so far as to suggest that everybody has struggled with some type of bad habit or compulsive behavior. Dr. Jonathan Chamberlain, formerly at Brigham Young University, called these "self-defeating behaviors"(1) He says it is a natural and normal part of growing up in an imperfect world to develop self-defeating behaviors. Even in the best of families, it is unavoidable that children will develop an "S.D.B". These range from relatively mild S.D.B.s to severe S.D.B.s that destroy lives. These self-defeating behaviors include such behaviors as over-eating, viewing pornography, compulsive lying, stealing, gambling, self-mutilation or cutting, using drugs and alcohol, throwing temper tantrums, isolating ourselves from others. These kinds of behaviors constitute what is referred to in the scriptures as the "chains of hell." These chains can progress to the point that they utterly enslave us and take away our free agency. As stated in 2 Nephi 1:13:

"O that ye would awake; awake from a deep sleep, yea, even from a deep sleep of hell, and shake off the awful chains by which ye are bound, which are the chains which bind the children of men, that they are carried away captive down to the eternal gulf of misery and woe."

   In most cases these self-defeating behaviors develop innocently enough. In a conference I attended many years ago. Dr. Chamberlain gave the following analogy. He said that suppose a boy had been asked to carry a trashcan outside to empty in the garbage. It is the middle of winter and there is snow on the ground. Some mean boys across the street begin throwing snowballs at the unfortunate boy. He discovers he can use his empty trashcan as a shield to block the snowballs. It works quite well and he is quite pleased with himself. It turns out this happens several times and he becomes quite adept at blocking snowballs with his trashcan. He becomes quite attached to this trashcan and very fond of it and even begins taking the trashcan to school. He gets teased and harassed by other students and becomes known as the trashcan boy. His parents, teachers and the principle are not happy with him for lugging this trashcan wherever he goes. It becomes burdensome to carry around this trash can everywhere but he is afraid to give it up. He feels safe and comfortable with his trashcan even though it has now become a liability to him. So it is with self-defeating behaviors. In the beginning, for example, it becomes quite comforting to eat sweet and fattening foods such as ice cream and cookies to cope with feelings such as discouragement, loneliness, or anxiety. After awhile, however, it becomes self-defeating to us and we become dangerously over weight. Virtually every one of us has developed at least one of these self-defeating behaviors. It becomes one of the major tasks of life to over come our self-defeating behaviors.

   Being active in the Church does not make us immune to S.D.B.s. I have counseled with many active, faithful members of the Church who have inadvertently developed very serious self-defeating behaviors. So serious they would constitute an addiction. Many people, for instance, develop a dependency on narcotics and pain killers that are legitimately prescribed for pain relief for injuries, illness, surgery, etc.; But people begin taking these drugs for other reasons besides pain relief i.e. to comfort themselves when they are feeling blue, fatigued, anxious or other negative feelings. With the Internet, sexual addiction to pornography has exploded in the Church as well as out side the Church. Pornography has become so readily available and accessible to our youth that many fall victim to these evil influences. It is so alluring and enticing that anyone could become entangled in this sin. Also, in the pressure to stay thin, many of our young women succumb to amphetamines. Methamphetamine use has skyrocketed in Utah as well as other places. The big problem with the use of these materials and substances is that even though they may provide temporary escape from stress and negative feelings and feel pleasurable and comforting, ultimately they become harmful and even deadly

All these self-defeating behaviors distance us from God and the Spirit. This is one of the most destructive consequences of S.D.B.s. It alienates us from our Heavenly Father, his Son and the Holy Ghost. Even the mildest addictions detract from the spirit at least temporarily. Other times addictions can become so severe that we are left utterly devoid of God and the spirit in our lives. We revert back to our natural godless selves and become as Peter said "natural brute beasts." (2 Peter 2:12) So many times we hear of horrendous crimes such as murder, child abuse, and rape being committed while a person is high on drugs or alcohol. In the same vein, pedophiles become addicted first to child pornography which oftentimes leads to molestation and heinous crimes against children. These crimes are committed by addicted people in whom the spirit is totally absent in their lives. David O. McKay defined spirituality as "consciousness of victory over self" It is one of the main goals in life to eliminate our S.D.Bs and bad habits. We then can gain this victory over our natural selves, feel of the spirit abundantly, and draw closer to God.

Treatment

Behavioral therapy techniques are particularly helpful in overcoming these addictions. Dr. Chamberlain asks his clients to keep diaries and write extensively how they do their self-defeating behaviors and in what circumstances and in what places. He asks them to identify all the prices or harmful consequences for doing their self-defeating behaviors. He also asks them to identify all the different triggers or precipitants to their self-defeating behaviors. These triggers could be just about anything. Like cigarette smoking triggers cancer, these triggers stimulate the growth of a cancer-like self-defeating behavior. A trigger could be an emotion such as anger, anxiety, stress or boredom. Or a trigger could be associating with certain friends with lower standards in precarious circumstances. Oftentimes a self-defeating behavior is done secretly and in private e.g. being alone late night when every body else has retired for the evening. This solitary time with your defenses down is a powerful trigger to the addictive behavior for many people.

Having identified your triggers you can then develop an alternative plan for dealing with these triggers other than engaging in your self-defeating behaviors. For example, a man who has an addiction to pornography on the Internet late at night when he is by himself may decide to not turn the computer on after a certain hour and instead retire to bed early. I had one such client who was able to over come his pornography addiction by merely going to bed with his wife at a reasonable hour and not staying up late by himself watching lustful TV programs. Journalizing, writing, identifying triggers and developing healthy, non-S.D.B. alternatives become an important part of recovery.

Part of every non-S.D.B. alternative plan is avoiding places where you will be tempted. This is what behavioral therapists call "stimulus control." A saying common in the alcohol and drug treatment field is, "If you have to be tough, you have not played it smart." It is not smart to deliberately place yourself in a situation where you must exercise a lot of will power. Sooner or later you will fall. No one is strong enough to knowingly put himself or herself in harm's way and not eventually succumb. A person with an alcohol addiction, for example, should not continually go to parties where alcohol is served. Even though he may tell himself that he is strong and that he can resist, eventually he will give in. It would be much better if he did not go anywhere near parties, bars, etc., where alcohol is readily available. The scriptures are replete with examples. Joseph, when tempted by Potiphar's wife, *ran*. He left the tempting situation as fast as humanly possible. He did not stay around to chat with her or allow her to tempt him. King David, on the other hand, saw the beautiful Bath-sheba bathing. He demurred and did not avert his eyes. Instead of running in the opposite direction and turning his attention elsewhere, he lusted after her. This led to his downfall. We need to literally run from temptation just as Joseph did and avoid those triggering situations as we would a terrible plague.

In overcoming self-defeating behaviors remember the three Ms to change. These are: Modifying your environment; Monitoring your progress; and Making a commitment. (2) In keeping with the example of a pornography addiction, modifying your environment would include disconnecting the Internet or getting a very good filtering system. Moving the computer to the living room or some other heavily frequented room where it would be very difficult to do this behavior in private would also be modifying the environment. It would, of course, also include avoiding the magazine section or video sections of stores. Monitoring your progress would include keeping a daily journal. It could also mean keeping track of every time you are tempted to view pornography and charting these temptations on a daily basis. One could do this, for example, by taking a penny out of your pocket every time you are tempted and putting it in another pocket and counting the pennies at the end of every day and marking this on a chart. Just the act of monitoring the behavior helps to decrease the behavior. Finally, making a commitment means you make some type of verbal or written commitment to another person such as a bishop or therapist that you are going to stop these behaviors. Regularly reporting on your progress to the bishop or counselor would be an important part of this process. Sometimes this is very helpful to do this in a group setting such as at a twelve-step sexual addicts anonymous meeting.

Cognitive therapy can also be very helpful in overcoming addictions. Addicts of every kind commit various cognitive errors. This would include all or nothing thinking. To use myself as an example, so many times I have started a diet or good eating plan and it goes along great until I have a minor slip. Perhaps I eat one piece of candy or one cookie. I begin to think "I've already blown it anyway so why not just blow it all the way" This leads to a binge. Rationalizations are also very common. "I've been good all week Its not going to hurt to eat this one piece of pie" "I don't want to offend my host so I will go ahead and eat dessert this time" "Its not fair that other people can eat what ever they want and seem to stay thin Why can't I eat whatever I want?" Blaming is also another popular technique for keeping an addiction alive. "Well it's my wife's fault for me slipping up. If she would just stop making desserts and leaving goodies around the house."

A relapse starts in the mind first. That is why it is so important to keep careful track of your thoughts when you are tempted. Doing thought records and daily journalizing will assist you in monitoring your thoughts. For every negative thought, you need to answer this thought with a rational, positive, life affirming thought that keeps you on track. For example: "I would sure like to have that piece of pie. It's not fair that other people seem to be able to eat whatever they want and stay thin but who says life is always fair? I just know I feel much better physically and emotionally when I don't over eat and when I stick to a healthy eating plan. I'm going to resist and feel good about making that decision."

The new buzz word in weight loss that surely has applicability to controlling all S.D.B.s is called "cognitive control" In healthy eating, you must be conscious of your eating choices all the time. This does not mean you must be obsessed with your eating habits but you must make conscious choices and be mindful all the time of your thoughts and eating decisions or you will surely slip back into old, unhealthy eating patterns. When your mind goes on "automatic pilot" is the time you will most certainly relapse, whether it be over-eating, drinking alcohol, viewing pornography on TV or the Internet or any self-defeating behavior. It is so easy to slip into our self-defeating thoughts and behaviors that it takes constant vigilance. This reminds one of Jesus' admonitions to his disciples to "watch and pray." Jesus told his disciples in the Garden of Gethsemane: "Watch and pray, that ye enter not into temptation: the spirit is indeed willing, but the flesh is weak" (Matt 26:41) In addition to daily prayer, watchfulness and supplication, keeping a daily diary or log can be very helpful in maintaining cognitive control

Another popular concept in the addictions field right now that certainly aids in stimulus control and cognitive control is "urge surfing." This concept suggests that urges and cravings to overeat, use drugs or alcohol, view pornography or perform any SDB come in waves. They are not continuous and the urges and cravings generally subside within a few minutes. Clients are encouraged to ride the cravings out and "surf the urge." During the time that you are "surfing the urge" you could recite a scripture or prayer, complete an unfinished task, or just relax in a hot bath. This concept is certainly compatible with gospel teachings. In James 4:7 we are counseled to "resist the devil and he will flee from you." We are frequently counseled by Church leaders to strenuously resist temptation when it comes upon us. This runs counter to the myth perpetuated by our culture that "if it feels good, do it!" Good moral character is developed by actively resisting destructive urges and cravings.

This brings me to a discussion of the twelve steps. I absolutely believe Bill W. in the 1950s was inspired from God when he developed the twelve steps. These steps are an integral part of Alcoholics Anonymous and now there are twelve step groups for over eaters, sexual addicts, gamblers and a host of other addictive behaviors. They have helped millions of people to over come addictions. These are the twelve steps:

1. We admitted to ourselves we were powerless over alcohol-that our live had become unmanageable.

2. Came to believe that a Power greater than ourselves could restore us to sanity.

3. Made a decision to turn our will and lives over to the care of God as we understood him.

4. Made a searching and fearless moral inventory of ourselves.

5. Admitted to God, to ourselves and to another human being the exact nature of our wrongs.

6. Were entirely ready to have God remove these defects of character.

7. Humbly asked Him to remove our shortcomings

8. Made a list of all persons we had harmed and became willing to make amends to them all.

9. Made direct amends to such people wherever possible, except when to do so would injure them or others.

10. Continued to take personal inventory and when we were wrong promptly admit it.

11. Sought through prayer and meditation to improve our conscious contact with God as we understood Him, praying only for knowledge of His will for us and the power to carry that out.

12. Having had a spiritual awakening as the result of these steps, we tried to carry this message to other alcoholics, and to practice these principles in all our affairs.

The first step involves getting past our denial and admitting we can no longer control our addictive behavior. It has become unmanageable in our lives. We are admitting we can no longer control this problem by ourselves. The second and third step involves believing there is a God and he has the power to save us. The fourth step involves taking a hard and courageous look at ourselves. We must humble ourselves before God and recognize all our weaknesses. The fifth step involves confession to God and another person, such as a priesthood leader. The sixth and seventh steps involve having faith and asking God to remove our weaknesses and make these weaknesses into strengths. The eighth and ninth steps involve making amends to the people we have harmed as a result of our addictive behavior. The tenth step merely means having a humble attitude and readily admitting when we have sinned or made a mistake. The eleventh step means trying to increase our involvement with God and the Spirit through regular prayer and other means. Finally, the twelfth step means that having been spiritually reborn we try to help others who are still struggling with addictive behaviors.

These twelve steps should look very familiar to L.D.S. people as they are basically the steps of repentance. This is the wonderful way the Lord has provided through the atonement for men and women to take full responsibility for their addictions and self-defeating behaviors and overcome them. The twelve steps are an effective formula for any of us to follow as we all suffer from some kind of self-defeating behavior.

There are A.A. meetings in virtually every city. I recommend to all my substance-abusing clients that they attend A.A. It typically takes months for people to work through all twelve steps. Other twelve step groups exist as well such as Over Eaters Anonymous and Sexual Addicts Anonymous. Even when it is impossible to attend a twelve-step meeting, it is important to work through these steps as thoroughly as possible with the assistance of a therapist or priesthood leader. With the assistance of A.A. and therapy I have known many people with severe addictions completely recover. God does not leave us hopeless. I am including at the end of this chapter the L.D.S. version of the twelve steps with scriptural references used at the L.D.S. Social Services Substance Abuse Recovery Groups.

Addictions and the Family

Now I wish to speak to the family members and those who are close to the addict. It is extremely common for family members to get caught in the snares of co-dependency. I recently spoke at a Relief Society fireside and talked about co-dependency and almost all the sisters could relate to it. I first learned about the co-dependency cycle from Melody Beattie (3) The co-dependency cycle of behavior occurs in families whenever there is a family member acting irresponsibly, such as a drug or alcohol abuser. Since teenagers do not always act responsibly, it often occurs in families where there is a teenager acting out. The cycle of co-dependency perpetuates the acting out behavior. There are three roles that exist in a co-dependency cycle. Typically one person, such as a spouse or parent, can easily fulfill all three roles. The roles are as follows:

1. Enabler or Rescuer - This is typically a parent or spouse who covers up and makes excuses for the

addict. He or she "rescues" the addict from the consequences of his or her own behavior. An example of this would be a dutiful wife calling the boss and telling the boss her husband is sick and cannot come into work when in reality he is drunk and hung over. In this fashion the addict never has to face the consequences of his own behavior.

2. Provoker or Persecutor - The family member is rescuing the addict but he or she is angry and hurt for being used. She typically nags scolds and argues with the addict. When a family member does this she is playing into the addict's hands. The addict uses this as an excuse to continue his irresponsible behavior. The addict often picks fights with his family members so he can have an excuse to place the entire blame on some one else. This excuses him (in his mind at least) to continue doing his self-defeating behavior.

3. Victim or Sufferer - This again is typically the parent or spouse. She suffers tremendous guilt and shame. She typically starts to believe the addict's words. "Maybe I am a failure as a wife or parent. It's my fault he does not come home on time. I am the one responsible for his drinking."

Something happens after the sufferer or victim is through beating him or herself up for the addict's problems. He or she resolves to do better and try harder. He or she tries fruitlessly to "fix" the addict once again and she begins the rescuing and enabling once more. Graphed this cycle would appear this way:

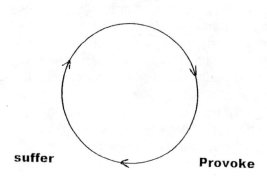

Rescue

suffer　　　　　　　　　　　　**Provoke**

    This co-dependency cycle is destructive to all those involved. It perpetuates the addict's irresponsible behavior. The co-dependent person often suffers from serious depression and guilt. Other family members are neglected and stand in the shadows while this cycle keeps repeating itself over and over again. To break out of this cycle requires three types of love (4)

Self-Love: The codependent individual usually suffers from the core beliefs of excessive responsibility and neglecting own needs. Their whole focus has been on "fixing" the addict. He or she loses touch with his or her own needs. They invariably suffer from depression and often have serious health problems. They must begin to focus on their own needs and begin taking care of themselves. This is a difficult process for them to do because they have neglected themselves for so long they do not even know what their needs are. They must, however, begin with the basics of getting enough sleep, eating properly, feeding themselves spiritually, exercising, and so forth. The world must become a friendly place again.

Tough Love: This involves setting limits and establishing good boundaries. They must stop the rescuing behavior. It is difficult to allow our loved ones to suffer but it must be done. Usually the only way an addict will consent to receive help is after much suffering. Sometimes this may even mean "creating a crisis" so the addict receives the opportunity to face the consequences of his behavior. For example, if a family member is aware that the addict is drinking and driving then she calls the police. This sounds like a cruel thing to do to our own family member but it is actually an act of love.

Unconditional Love: This needs to be explained thoroughly. A family can and should express their love to the addict but only in "safe ways" This means family members can tell the addict they love him and perhaps even give him a hug or a special note but no rescuing. The family member assures the addict of his love but they must step back and allow the suffering to occur. Like the prodigal son, when the addict finally "comes to his senses" they welcome him back with open arms but not before he has entered treatment and initiated serious, long term changes. Promises are not enough. He must show through persistent effort that he is very serious about making these changes.

Since this co-dependency cycle is so common, the three types of love need to be practiced in all families to a certain extent. We need to stand ready to help a family member in need but we also need to know when we should step back and allow the family member to face the consequences alone. I liken it to when we first helped our precious children learn how to ride a bicycle. There are times when we as parents will run along aside the child and steady the bicycle. But other times we must also know when to let go and let the child struggle on his own. The child may even crash but we as parents know that a crash or two is inevitable when learning to ride a bike. We are there to quell the tears. However, we still allow the child to make mistakes and learn from those mistakes.

In the next chapter I will be talking in detail about other factors that contribute to mental and emotional problems such as biology and environment.

———————

THE TWELVE-STEPS used by LDS Substance Abuse Recovery Groups

1.   We admitted we were powerless over compulsive/addictive behaviors (*any behavior may be inserted here*)—that our lives had become unmanageable. **Admitted that we of ourselves are powerless, nothing without God.** *(Mosiah 4:5; Alma 26:12)*

2. Came to believe that a Power greater than ourselves could restore us to sanity. **Came to believe that God has all power and all wisdom and that in His strength we can do all things.** *(Mosiah 4:9; Alma 26:12)*

3. Made a decision to turn our will and our lives over to the care of God as we understood Him. **Made the decision to reconcile ourselves to the will of God, offer our whole souls as an offering unto Him, and trust Him in all things forever.** *(2 Nephi 3:34, 10:24; Omni 1:26; Mosiah 3:19)*

4. Made a searching and fearless moral inventory of ourselves. **Made a searching and fearless written inventory of our past in order to thoroughly examine ourselves as to our pride and other**

weaknesses with the intent of recognizing our own carnal state and our need for Christ's Atonement. *(Mosiah 4:2; Alma 15:17; Jacob 4:6)*

5. Admitted to God, to ourselves and to another human being the exact nature of our wrongs. **Honestly shared this inventory with God and with another person, thus demonstrating the sincerity of our repentance, and our willingness to give away all our sins that we might know Him.** *(Mosiah 26:29; Alma 22:18)*

6. Were entirely ready to have God remove all these defects of character. **Became humble enough to yield our hearts and our lives to Christ for His sanctification and purification, relying wholly upon His merits, acknow-ledging even our own best efforts as unpro-fitable.** *(Helaman 3:35; 2 Nephi 31:19; Mosiah 20:21)*

7. **Humbly asked Him to remove our shortcomings. Humbly cried unto the Lord Jesus Christ in our hearts for a remission of sins that through His mercy and His grace we might experience a mighty change of heart, lose all disposition to do evil, and thus be encircled about in the arms of safety because of His great and last sacrifice.** *(Alma 34:15-16; 36:18; 38:8; Moroni 10:32; Mosiah 5:2)*

8. Made a list of all persons we had harmed and became willing to make amends to them all. **Made a list of all persons we had harmed and became willing to make restitution to all of them (even those we had harmed in what we might consider righteous anger,) desiring instead to be peacemakers and to do all that we could to come unto God by first being reconciled to others.** *(3 Nephi 12:9; 24:41-45)*

9. Made direct amends to such other people wherever possible except when to do so would injure them or others. **Made restitution directly to those we had harmed, confessing our own wrongdoing in each instance except when to do so would further injure them or others.** *(Mosiah 26:30; 27:35; 3 Nephi 12:25)*

10. Continued to take personal inventory and when wrong, promptly admitted it. **Realizing that the weakness to be tempted and to sin is a part of the mortal experience, we continued to take personal inventory and when we were wrong promptly admitted it, being willing to repent as often as needed.** *(2 Nephi 4:18; 10:20; Mosiah 26:30)*

11. Sought through prayer and meditation to improve our conscious contact with God as we understood Him, praying only for knowledge of His will for us and the power to carry that out. **Sought through prayer and meditation to improve our conscious communication with God, seeking the words of Christ through the power of the Holy Ghost that they might tell us all things that we should do, praying only for a knowledge of His will for us and the power to carry that out.** *(2 Nephi 32:3; Alma 37:37; Helaman 10:4)*

12. Having had a spiritual awakening as the result of these steps, we tried to carry this message to others still suffering from the effects of compulsive behaviors and to practice these principles in all our affairs. **Having experienced a mighty change and having awakened unto God as a result of our sincere repentance demonstrated in taking these steps, we were willing to become instruments in carrying this message to others and to practice these principles in all our affairs.** *(Alma 5:7; Mosiah 27:26, 27; Moroni 7:3)*

CHAPTER 12

Other factors

So far I have emphasized how beliefs and thoughts cause depression, anxiety and other emotional problems. It is undeniable that other factors contribute as well. Several years ago I attended a workshop by Drs. Michael Lowery and Candace Lowery of Wasatch Hospital in Salt Lake City. They presented the interactional model for depression. (1) According to this model, three factors contribute to depression: biology, environment and psychology and these factors interact with each other. Diagrammed the model appears this way:

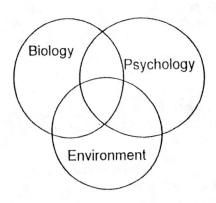

Depending on the person, the circles on this chart can vary. For instance, for one person the biological factor may be more of a factor. For another individual, environment may play a bigger role than the other two factors. For every body all three factors contribute in some fashion and they interact and exacerbate each other. I will describe each factor in some detail.

Biology- I am not a physician so I will not attempt to describe in exact detail how biological factors contribute to depression and other emotional illnesses. However, genetics and biological factors definitely contribute to emotional and mental disorders. Depression, for instance, is just as much a medical illness as diabetes or cancer. In relation to depression, certain chemicals in the brain called neurotransmitters pass from neuron to neuron. They must cross the gap between neurons called synapses. Certain neurotransmitters such as serotonin and norepinephrine are key in regulating emotional responses. When there are deficiencies in these chemicals and not enough are crossing the synaptic gap then depression and other emotional illnesses usually occur. A category of drugs called SSRIs (Selective Serotonin Reuptake Inhibitors) such as Prozac, Paxil and Zoloft assure that enough serotonin is crossing the synapses. These medications are not "happy pills" and are not addictive. No one goes to parties to get "high" on Prozac and other anti-depressants. They merely restore the neurotrans-mitters to normal levels so that sufferers can feel normal once more. I also do not believe that anti-depressants change personalities. They help us to feel normal once again and normal for someone who has been feeling depressed or severely anxious feels marvelous. These medications, in my opinion, are gifts from God. We should be grateful for them. However, they are not the full story and the only treatment for emotional ills as some pharmaceutical companies would have you believe.

Genetics is also a factor and depression and

several other mental disorders tend to run in families. If both of your parents suffer from depression, for example, then you have a greater genetic *predisposition* to depression. This does not mean you are destined to become depressed but you are more predisposed.

Certain hormones and vitamins can also be contributors. Hypothyroidism, for instance, can appear much like clinical depression. Vitamin B6 deficiency can produce the same results. Therefore, it always a good idea to be examined by a physician when you are suffering from severe depressive symptoms or severe anxiety. Even severe anger can sometimes be ameliorated through medications. It is not a sign a weakness to take psychotropic medications any more than it is for a diabetic to take insulin. But just as exercising and maintaining a healthy diet can do much to control diabetes, there is a lot you can do to control these emotional illnesses.

Environment- This refers to what is happening in our environment to cause us stress. Whether it is due to marital, financial, vocational or other social problems, stress is a fact of life and unavoidable. Too much stress over long periods of time can take a toll on anyone. Recently I had a client whose husband had died, and she lost her house and employment all within three months. How could anyone not be adversely affected by so much stress? Just as stress can contribute to hypertension, headaches, abdominal pain, etc., it can also contribute to depression and anxiety. Psychologists such as Holmes and Rahe say that too much stress and change in anyone's life will negatively affect their health. Even so called happy events such as a child getting married can be very stressful. They have developed a stress index which predicts how likely you will develop health problems based on the degree of change and stress occurring in your life.. I am including their index at the end of this chapter for your perusal. This index does not guarantee with absolute certainty that you will get sick or depressed but just how *likely* you are to become sick or depressed.

Another environmental factor that I would like to mention in detail is loss. Loss typically leads to grief and bereavement which can very much look like depression. However, with grief there is not usually the loss of self-worth and suicidal thoughts that often accompany depression. It is completely normal to have crying spells, insomnia, loss of appetite and other physical symptoms following a severe loss. These physical symptoms do not usually last longer than two months (2) Grief, depending on how it is handled, can lead to clinical depression. I know of two sisters, for instance, who are approximately the same age and both lost their husbands around the same time. They were both grief stricken. One sister, as to be expected, felt sadness at the passing of her husband but she reached out to others for support. She did not suffer alone. She also attempted to stay busy and active. She found something else to bring meaning to her life and became involved in temple work. She branched out and developed a new set of friends. After several months she successfully resolved her grief. Certainly she misses her husband but she is living a happy, very fulfilled life. The other sister is another story. She became withdrawn after the death of her husband. She became isolated and would go days without hardly seeing another soul. She lost her job which added to her isolation and she lacked constructive activities. Her grief developed into a severe depression which lasted for three years. She is just now finally coming out to church and getting more socially involved. She has recently obtained part time employment. She is finally coming out of her depression but it persisted for years and significantly contributed to her suffering.

In the process of working through grief it is helpful to remember the stages of grief by Dr. J. William Worden. (3) He says the first step to successful grieving is *accepting the reality of the loss*. Most people are understandably in shock when they first learn of the loss, whether it be the loss of a family member, a job, etc; They often can be heard saying: "I can't believe this has happened" They may try to avoid this stage by refusing to talk about it. However, they must finally accept the reality of the loss before they can move onto the next stage which is *experience the pain*. Many people try to avoid this stage by numbing themselves with alcohol, drugs, etc.; however, you must allow yourself to "sit in the pain". This means having many good cries and allowing yourself to truly mourn. It can take many months and even years for the pain to go away altogether. Even then anniversaries and special events occur that remind you of the loss and it is normal to feel sad. The third stage of successful grieving according to Dr. Worden is *adjusting to the environment*. For example, when a close family member dies you will have to make adjustments and learn new skills. When a wife loses a husband, for instance, she must do things for herself that her husband typically did, such as paying the bills, taking care of the lawn, or taking care of the vehicles. Sometimes severe adjustments have to be made such as when a widow has to find a job and support her family financially. Finally the last stage to successful grieving is *withdrawing emotional energy from the loss and re-investing it*. This is the stage when a person finally must move on and find meaning in her life despite the loss. In the above example, the widow re-invested her energy from the grieving and loss and put it in temple work which became very satisfying and rewarding to her. It is not that she forgot her husband but she found joy and happiness in her life once more.

Certain people who have dysfunctional core beliefs are more vulnerable to stress and contribute to their own stress by their negative thoughts. Core beliefs such as perfectionism, excessive responsibility and neglecting our own needs certainly make people more susceptible to the negative effects of stress. Effective stress management, in addition to relaxation techniques, usually requires changes in attitude and beliefs.

Psychology-This refers to attitudes and beliefs that contribute to depression. I will not spend time here talking about psychology since essentially this whole book addresses this topic. I do want to emphasize that unless a person gets help in this area his or her depression is likely to return. A person who only takes medications for depression, for instance, has not changed his core beliefs and his way of thinking. As soon as he discontinues the medications, he is likely to return to his depression. Research bears out that therapy and medications together are the best course of treatment for depression, severe anxiety and other emotional disorders for most people.

I would like to include another circle in the interactional model for depression. It appears this way:

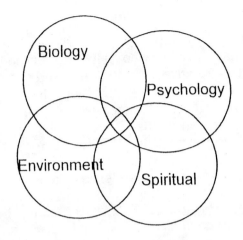

    I fervently believe that spiritual factors contribute to depression just as much as biological, environmental, and psychological factors. Those who are lacking the Spirit in their lives are more vulnerable to depression and other emotional disorders. It is all part of a complex, interacting web. We must take care of ourselves in all four areas to become completely whole. If we are lacking in one area it will surely affect us in the other three areas. We must do what we can to take care of our physical health, minimize and manage environmental stress, develop healthy beliefs and attitudes and feed ourselves spiritually. To paraphrase the sermon on the mount, when we are built upon this rock we will not fail. The rains may descend and fierce winds may blow but we will remain safe and secure on this sure foundation.

LIFE CHANGE INDEX SCALE
by Thomas H. Holmes

*(To help you identify some of the stresses in your life, the following scale cites positive and negative life events. Each is rated according to the amount of adjustment needed to cope with them. To use the scale, add up the life changes you have experienced **within the past year** and place the total on the line at the end of the scale.)*

1	Death of spouse	1 _____	100
2	Divorce	2 _____	73
3	Marital separation from mate	3 _____	65
4	Detention in jail or other institution	4 _____	63
5	Death of a close family member	5 _____	63
6	Major personal injury or illness	6 _____	53
7	Marriage	7 _____	60
8	Being fired at work	8 _____	47
9	Marital reconciliation	9 _____	45
10	Retirement from work	10 _____	45
11	Major change in health or behavior of a family member	11 _____	44
12	Pregnancy	12 _____	40
13	Sexual difficulties	13 _____	39
14	Gaining a new family member (e.g., through birth, adoption, oldster moving in, etc.)	14 _____	39
15	Major business readjustment (e.g., merger, reorganization, bankruptcy, etc.)	15 _____	38
16	Major change in financial state (e.g., either a lot worse off or a lot better off than usual)	16 _____	37
17	Death of a close friend	17 _____	36
18	Changing to a different line of work	18 _____	36

19 Major change in the number of arguments with spouse (e.g., either a lot more or a lot less than usual regarding child-rearing, personal habits, etc.)   19 _____ 25

20 Taking on a mortgage greater than $10,000 (e.g., purchasing a home, business, etc.)   20 _____ 31

21 Foreclosure on a mortgage or loan   21 _____ 30

22 Major change in responsibilities at work (e.g., promotion, demotion, lateral transfer)   22 _____ 29

23 Son or daughter leaving home (e.g., marriage, attending college, etc.)   23 _____ 29

24 In-law troubles   24 _____ 29

25 Outstanding personal achievement   25 _____ 28

26 Spouse beginning or ceasing work outside the home   26 _____ 26

27 Beginning or ceasing formal schooling   27 _____ 26

28 Major change in living conditions (e.g., building a new home, remodeling, deterioration of home or neighborhood)   28 _____ 25

29 Revision of personal habits (dress, manners, associations, etc.)   29 _____ 24

30 Troubles with the boss   30 _____ 23

31 Major change in working hours or conditions   31 _____ 20

32 Change in residence   32 _____ 20

33 Changing to a new school   33 _____ 20

34 Major change in usual type and/or amount of recreation   34 _____ 19

35 Major change in church activities (e.g., a lot more or a lot less than usual)   35 _____ 19

36 Major change in social activities (e.g., clubs, dancing, movies, visiting, etc.)   36 _____ 18

37 Taking on a mortgage or loan less than $10,000 (e.g., purchasing a car, TV, freezer, etc.)	37 _____	17
38 Major change in sleeping habits (a lot more or a lot less sleep or change in time of day when asleep)	38 _____	16
39 Major change in number of family get-togethers (e.g., a lot more or a lot less than usual)	39 _____	15
40 Major change in eating habits (a lot more or a lot less food intake, or very different meal hours or surroundings)	40 _____	15
41 Vacation	41 _____	13
42 Christmas	42 _____	12
43 Minor violations of the law (e.g., traffic tickets, jaywalking, disturbing the peace, etc.)	43 _____	11

Total Life Change Units (LCU) _____

Interpreting your score

0-150	No significant problem
150-199	Mild Life Crisis Level with a 35% chance of illness
200-299	Moderate Life Crisis Level with a 50% chance of illness
300 or over	Major Life Crisis Level with an 80% chance of illness

CHAPTER 13

Day by day

In this chapter I will be discussing how to implement therapy and spirituality on a daily basis. A complaint I often hear from people, especially from adolescence, is "I'm having a bad day!" I believe I was guilty of saying that myself when I was a teenager. People describe their moods as some strange, alien force that comes over them over which they have absolutely no control. It reminds me of the old TV shows and movies where some unfortunate individual is hypnotized by the evil professor. The hypnotized individual has a weird, glazed look in his eyes and he is compelled to do behaviors against his will. In the same way, some people seem to react as though their moods and feelings are some alien force that has overcome their minds and bodies over which they have no control. Until such people realize they do have control over their moods and feelings, they will continue to suffer from depression, severe anxiety and other emotional ills. We create our negative feelings and we can learn to dispel them.

It takes consistent and daily practice for people to gain control over their feelings and moods. There will be setbacks but one must not give up or give into despair and hopelessness. I have discussed often the importance of doing Thought Records. In the beginning, these records should be done a daily basis. It will help the sufferer to gain eventual control over his depression, anxiety and anger. As mentioned in previous chapters, this can be as simple as drawing a line down the middle of a paper and in one column writing down his negative, "automatic thoughts". In the other column, the person counters the negative thoughts with more realistic, positive thoughts. The person attempts to look at the situation in the most rational and objective way he can. He tries to look at the situation the way his best friend or loved one would look at the situation. He then writes this "Rational Response" in the other column. This is commonly called the double column technique. (1) It takes daily practice but eventually the individual can break the train of negative, habitual thinking. This leads to a greatly improved mood and happiness. The following is an example of a double-column exercise:

Automatic Thoughts	Rational Response
I made a complete idiot of myself today when I taught that Relief Society class. I fumbled over my words and nobody got anything useful or inspirational at all from my class. They will never ask me to do that again.	I made some minor errors but overall I got my points across. There were several sisters who seemed to be interested and made some good comments. I got a couple of compliments after the class from Sister Jones and Sister Smith. I'm new at this but overall it was a good first effort. I would be happy to try again if they ask.

We also need to strengthen our new core beliefs on a daily basis. If, for instance, a person is trying to strengthen a new belief that says: "I'm a person of high worth. I am equal to anyone and I am succeeding with the talents and strengths the Lord has blessed me with;" everyday that person will write down at least three things he did on a daily log that confirms this new belief. Even if these achievements seem small and insignificant it should be written down anyway. Since depressed people tend to discount the positive or minimize positive experiences and evidence, it is very important that the person write down everything that happened that day that seemed to confirm the new belief. Eventually that person will start to *believe* the new belief and this will lead to new-found confidence and self-esteem.

Another way to strengthen a new belief on a daily basis is to act on the new belief. An example of this would be a person who is trying to establish the new core belief: "I must take care of my own needs first before giving to others" This new belief can be strengthened by acting on the new belief and taking an hour for himself everyday and refusing to feel guilty about it. He must constantly remind himself that even though this is a lot of time he is worth it and this is a valuable investment in himself (or herself.) Eventually the person will not feel guilty about taking some time to himself everyday.

Recently I attended a conference on spirituality and healing and one of the presenters was Dr. N. Lee Smith of the University of Utah. (2) He talked about how prevalent depression and anxiety are with those suffering from medical problems and physical pain. He said that at least 38 to 42% of people who visit a medical doctor infrequently (less than five times in a year) suffer from underlying depression and anxiety. However, of those who visit a physician frequently (more than twenty times a year) virtually a 100% of them suffer from depression and anxiety. Depression and anxiety are huge contributors to medical problems and physical pain. Such people who suffer from frequent pain and sickness and who visit medical personnel frequently usually lack four characteristics in their lives i.e. a sense of personal control, a sense of connectedness with others and God, a sense of purpose and meaning, and hope. These are four qualities we all need to cultivate in our lives on a daily basis. Dr. Smith says these four qualities can be provided by spirituality, regular church attendance and religious worship.

Dr. Smith gives four steps to help people develop a sense of personal control that can easily be adapted to cognitive therapy and could be practiced on a daily basis. He began by saying:

1. Become consciously aware (e.g. write down your automatic thoughts in a particular situation)

2. Relax (perhaps do some deep breathing, meditation, scripture reading)

3. Clarify your deep values (e.g. write down your positive thoughts and how you want to be in a particular situation)

4. Visualize (imagine yourself acting in the new way according to your new beliefs and values)

You are then ready to step into reality and act in a new, more productive way and you will feel a sense of personal power and control. Dr. Smith, who is an internist, says that when people have a sense of control then neurotransmitters, such as serotonin and dopamine, actually increase. Illnesses such as fibromyalgia, irritable bowel syndrome and chronic fatigue syndrome improve and sufferers experience a better quality of life.

Spirituality also needs to be practiced on a daily basis in addition to these cognitive and behavioral techniques. Going to church once a week or less is not enough. To fight against the daily onslaught of carnal, lustful influences requires us to charge our spiritual batteries daily. We need to exercise our spiritual muscles daily for the worldly, carnal bully, who is constantly lurking in the shadows, will frequently attempt to overpower us. It is essential that we practice spirituality everyday in some fashion e.g. reading scriptures, praying, meditating and pondering, taking peaceful walks in nature, service, etc. to remain strong against the "fiery darts of the evil one"

A technique that I have taught many clients over the years that promotes peace, serenity and spirituality is called the Relaxation Response.(3) This is a daily meditative technique developed by Dr. Herbert Benson of Harvard. He says it is not necessary to delve into Eastern philosophy and, in fact, you can adapt this technique to any religion you belong to. It is easy to learn and comprises of the following steps:

1. Choose a focus word or phrase (seven words or less) such as a scripture or word such as peace or calm.

2. Relax your muscles as deeply as possible

3. Repeat your focus word or phrase to yourself every time you exhale.

4. When your mind wanders then simply say to yourself "Oh well" and gently return to focusing on your word or phrase. Don't worry about whether you are doing the

technique correctly. Keep a passive attitude and "go with the flow" Become an observer to your own thoughts and practice letting them go.

He suggests you do this technique once or twice daily for 10-20 minutes. I found this technique very relaxing and calming. I look forward to doing it every day and it is a great method for clearing your mind. I often feel the Holy Ghost while doing this technique. I have found it wonderful preparation for prayer for it gets your mind off of your daily worries and cares and helps you stay focused in the present moment. I usually pray immediately after doing this technique. It seems to make my prayers more sincere and heartfelt.

This is an example of things that can be done on a daily basis to become "spiritually grounded" Just like the Daily Requirement of Vitamins and Minerals developed by the federal government, I have developed my own Daily Requirement of Spiritual and Healthy Practices. For me this consists of

1. Reading scriptures daily for at least ten minutes individually and as a family

2. Praying twice daily including daily family prayer

3. Meditation for 10-20 minutes a day.

Although these are not strictly spiritual practices I also do the following:

4. Exercise 4-5 times a week (almost daily) which consists of strength training, riding a stationary bike or running and walking

5. Doing something fun and recreational for at least 15

minutes a day (for me this usually is reading a novel.) This one can certainly be over done but I have found that most people don't have enough time for fun.

6. Get 7-8 hour of sleep a night

Also there are things that I do on a weekly basis:

7. Do something recreational and fun with my wife and children for two hours

8. Family home evening

9. Go to church

10. Write in my journal

Also there are monthly activities:

11. Fast

12. Go to the temple

    We all need to do similar activities on a daily, weekly and monthly basis. Behavioral therapists call this activity scheduling and is a valuable treatment for depression. Typically depressed individuals lose their motivation and are constantly tired. They often spend their days sleeping, watching TV and other low energy, passive activities that do not engage their talents and skills. The more they give into "nothingism" the more depressed they become and this becomes a very destructive cycle. Part of the treatment for depression is scheduling an ideal, activity filled day for sufferers to follow and doing every thing possible to get these individuals to follow their schedules. They invariably feel better when they do. Cognitive therapists also like activity scheduling. It is like cognitive therapy in reverse. Instead of positive thoughts triggering positive behaviors, activity scheduling is positive behaviors triggering positive thoughts. Even though a person may have negative thoughts that this activity is not going to help, he is induced to do it anyway. Changing the behavior and "going through the motions" almost always triggers positive cognition. I believe this is what is meant by the scripture in Proverbs which states: "Commit thy works unto the Lord, and thy thoughts shall be established." (Proverbs 16:3) I have discovered this often with my exercising. There are many days when I do not feel like exercising and I tell myself it is not going to help. However, I still do it and I always feel better when I do and it improves my attitude and thinking as well.

Establishing my daily, weekly and monthly schedule in my life did not come easily. I had several bad habits and self-defeating behaviors that I had to root out. Happiness does not automatically come into a person's life. It requires that we all work to rid ourselves of our self-defeating habits that we unconsciously do every day. We must seek to replace the bad habits- including negative, automatic thinking- with healthy, life affirming habits. What more is life than a collection of habits - both good and bad - that we all do every day? Once we painstakingly alter and abolish our bad habits and replace them with daily, positive habits we will find ourselves being much happier. We usually can not rid ourselves of our bad habits on our own .It usually requires the help of another trusted person, such as a family member, friend, priesthood leader or therapist and, of course, the help of God.

A study conducted in 1998 by BYU sociologists Brent Top and Bruce Chadwick confirms the need for daily spiritual practices.(4)The researchers asked over

3,000 LDS adolescents about their participation in delinquent activities e.g. fighting, sex, drinking, smoking, stealing, etc. They also asked the youth about factors such as peer influence, family influence and "public religiosity" and "private religiosity" and how these factors either deterred or contributed to delinquency. By "public religiosity" they meant church attendance and the social aspects of church and "private religiosity" was defined as private prayer, private scripture study and fasting. They found that overall the youth of the Church had lower rates of delinquency when compared to non-LDS youth and that all these factors helped to deter delinquency in our youth. However, they said the most significant factor that appeared to lower delinquency was "private religiosity" or daily practices of private prayer and scripture study. There is much parents can do to encourage this private religious behavior in our youth. Not the least is setting a good example by doing these behaviors ourselves and also holding family prayer and scripture study. If these daily habits are important to youth they are certainly important to us adults as well. Attending church is important and edifying but daily wholesome, spiritual habits are what really fortify us against degrading worldly influences and produce true happiness.

Once a person has established a healthy daily routine inevitably a life stress will come along that will throw us off our daily routine. Perhaps this unpredicted stress will also lead into a relapse and we will commit a self-defeating behavior that we thought we had long ago conquered. Many people consequently think "all or nothing" thoughts that all is lost. This causes feelings of hopelessness and leads them to giving up. Dr. Pamela Peeke talks about the very important ability to "regroup" She says once we have established a good, life-affirming routine, it is certain that something will come along that will cause us to veer off track. She says that we should not despair. We need to have a "Plan B" ready that we can follow until we can get back on track. As an example, lets say you have been faithfully reading scriptures, praying, and exercising on a daily basis and your job suddenly requires you to work over time, which interferes with your schedule. Dr. Peeks says don't give up your healthy life style that you have worked so hard to establish. Do not go back to old self-destructive ways of thinking and behaving. Come up with a Plan B. Perhaps this will require you to exercise at night instead of in the morning. Maybe you and your family will temporarily have family prayer after dinner instead of in the morning. Dr. Peek also says to expect set backs and do not beat yourself up mentally if you slip. Be gentle with yourself and regroup. (5)

This regrouping is similar to the repentance process. We have been counseled to repent often, even on a daily basis. This daily repenting should not include berating ourselves and condemning ourselves. Peter asked the Savior how often we should forgive our neighbor. "Even seven times," he asked? His response was seventy times seven. (Matt 18:21-22) I believe strongly this admonition includes forgiving ourselves. We may have to repent and regroup seventy times seven before we have finally over come a self-defeating behavior and established a healthy habit in its place.

Doing these types of activities on a regular daily basis will not detract or interfere with your work and other duties but will actually help you to be more efficient. It will also help you perform better in your church calling. You will feel more rested and energetic and the time you do spend at work or on your calling will be more focused. This is what Stephen Covey calls "Sharpening the Saw" and is one of the habits of a highly effective person. Just as a dull saw wastes a lot of time and causes much frustration, we must take time to sharpen our saw daily to prevent us from becoming "dull." (6) If you do not have time for such daily activities then you are too busy. It may be that you will need to start setting limits with others and say "no" more often. This kind of balance in a person's life makes life full, joyful and rewarding.

CHAPTER 14

Trials

It would not be appropriate to finish this book before writing about trials. Earlier in this book, I mentioned it was never appropriate to experience depression. However, every man and every woman at some time in his or her life experiences a severe trial. This comes in many forms from a serious illness, such as cancer, to a wayward son or daughter. One may wonder if it is ever appropriate to feel heart broken and down trodden when we are beset with severe trials. It is not our destiny to suffer endless suffering and despair, but it is most certainly appropriate and normal to have periods of emotional pain and discouragement in our lives. How you choose to deal with these severe trials will determine whether these trials become stepping-stones to greater growth and fulfillment or whether these trials become stumbling blocks that weaken or even destroy you. .

The concepts presented in this book about cognitive therapy are never more valid than when you are confronted with a severe test. Attitude can make all the difference. Let us say that a man just discovered that he has cancer. His attitude could be the difference between life or death. Numerous studies have shown how important a positive attitude is in fighting illness. Our man could interpret this diagnosis of cancer as a death sentence. He could think: "That's it. My life is over" The man could sink into a depression and never recover. The cancer, fueled by his depression, would eventually take his life. However, that same man could interpret his diagnosis in this way: "This is a severe set back. This is very frightening and discouraging. However, I am going to fight this with every fiber of my being and I will conquer this!" This positive attitude will greatly augment his medical treatment and will aid in his recovery. There may be a time when the illness becomes so severe that he will have to accept that he will never get better. However, his attitude will determine whether he dies in peace or in bitterness and despair.

Most of the trials and challenges in our lives we do survive. However, these trials can either weaken and embitter us or they can ultimately strengthen us and make our lives more joyful. It is all up to us. When I was in my mission in Germany, I often talked to the older people of that country. These people had gone through tremendous suffering in two world wars. I noticed a pattern. Some of these elderly folks had become very bitter and angry. They had become extremely negative and saw no good to life whatsoever. They had been consumed with their bitterness. Other survivors, however, became kinder and more loving. Their trials had only increased their faith. They seemed to become eternal optimists. They were truly happy and a joy to associate with. I often wondered why some of these survivors of two world wars had become so depressed and embittered while others became more faithful and happy.

With the passing of the years, I have discovered the essential ingredient to successful coping with severe trials and suffering. I have discovered why some become angry and depressed while others seem to thrive as the result of their trials. The essential ingredient for successful coping is meaning and hope. Those who find meaning in their suffering are vaulted to greater heights. They adopt an attitude that they will learn and grow as a result of this trial no matter how bad it gets. They eventually go on to greater joy and happiness. They also hold on to hope no matter what the trial presents. They never give up hope no matter how grave and discouraging the challenge is and how much suffering they are required to endure.

Viktor Frankl, a German psychiatrist, was an inspiration to me early in my career. He developed a therapy around the importance of meaning called logotherapy. According to his therapy, it is not suffering that destroys people but suffering without meaning. Dr. Frankl is a German Jew and was imprisoned in a Nazi concentration camp. His parents, brother and wife all died in a concentration camp from starvation and hardships or were sent to the gas chamber. Dr. Frankl also endured horrible hardships in the form of starvation, beatings, and degradation before he was finally liberated in 1945. He noticed that only the concentration camp prisoners who were able to attach meaning to their suffering were able to survive that terrible ordeal. He said those who had "give-up-itis" would simply throw themselves on the fence and were shot, or they stayed in their beds and refused to get up. Within forty-eight hours they invariably died. Only those who could find some type of meaning in their suffering in the form of God, their family, their unfinished work, etc. were able to survive. He says that even in the most horrendous circumstances there is one freedom that cannot be robbed and that is our freedom to "choose one's attitude in a given set of circumstances" (1)

Dr. Frankl developed logotherapy from his experiences in the concentration camp. "Logo" comes from the Greek word "meaning" and he says those who develop a neurosis often lack meaning in their lives. He says the "will to meaning" is the strongest motivation in life. Many in our society have not discovered meaning and are floundering, especially many of our youth. We develop meaning in three ways. First, we can develop meaning through our work and our deeds. Secondly, he says we can develop meaning through love. Lastly, he says we develop meaning through our sufferings. Deriving meaning through our sufferings in turn helps us to endure the suffering.

He gives an uplifting example of this final step with the story of Jerry Long of Texas. Jerry broke his neck in a diving accident when he was age 17. He is quadriplegic now but his accident certainly did not destroy his spirit. He types with his mouth stick. He attends college classes and participates in class discussions. He is excited about getting a degree in psychology. His life is full of purpose and meaning. Jerry says that his personal credo is "I broke my neck, it didn't break me."(2)

The gospel teaches us similar concepts. The gospel gives meaning to our suffering. The gospel helps us to endure suffering and ultimately transcend the suffering. Through our sufferings, God can actually convert our suffering to our benefit. The scriptures are replete of examples of courageous, faithful men and women who endured suffering well and were blessed and strengthened by their suffering. Job, Joseph, Ruth, Alma, Amulek, Joseph Smith and many others in the scriptures endured their sufferings with faith and were blessed. After their suffering transformed them, they became instruments in God's hands and were able to help a multitude of people. Paul, in particular, talks about the purpose of suffering and of his "thorn in the flesh." He says:

"And lest I should be exalted above measure through the abundance of the revelations, there was given to me a thorn in the flesh, the messenger of Satan to buffet me, lest I should be exalted above measure. For this thing I besought the Lord thrice, that it might depart from me. And he said unto me, My grace is sufficient for thee: for my strength is made perfect in weakness. Most gladly therefore will I rather glory in my infirmities, that the power of Christ may rest upon me. Therefore I take pleasure in infirmities, in reproaches, in necessities, in persecutions, in distresses for Christ's sake: for when I am weak, then am I strong." (2 Cor 12: 7-10)

Can you imagine actually thanking and praising God for your infirmities and trials as Paul did? This would require much faith. We have all been "blessed" with some type of "thorn in the flesh". While you are going through this suffering and trial it is difficult to see it as a blessing but it certainly can be. You must be humble and open-minded during these times and ask God what He wants you to learn during these difficult periods. This often requires a shift in perception and a change in attitude for many people. Instead of looking at the trial as a barrier and punishment, you must look at the trial as a learning and growing opportunity. You also need to ask God for the courage and strength to endure this trial well. I have had some trials in my life and even though I do not wish to repeat them, I do thank God for the learning and knowledge I acquired through these trials. I believe I have learned more from my trials and hard times than from all the college classes I have ever taken. These trials did not last forever but they were tremendously beneficial to me in many ways.

During the difficult times it is important that you look for solutions. This often involves humbling yourself and asking for help. You must never give up hope. Hopelessness is the hallmark and number one symptom of depression. If you give up hope then you most assuredly will become depressed. This is not a condition that will help you to fight and over come your trials. It is appropriate and even healthy to feel temporary shock, profound sadness, hurt, anger, and fear but you cannot afford to give into hopelessness and depression. In a sense, if you give into hopelessness you are denying Christ. As Paul said Christ is our hope. (1 Timothy 1:1) Through Christ and his atonement and resurrection you can face anything, even death itself, with hope. The prophet Ether said this eloquently when he said:

"Wherefore, whoso believeth in God might with surety hope for a better world, yea, even a place at the right hand of God, which hope cometh of faith, maketh an anchor to the souls of men, which would make them sure and steadfast; always abounding in good works, being led to glorify God." (Ether 12: 4)

The importance of hope in any circumstance was reinforced to me in a speech presented by Dr. Christina Puchalski. (3) This internist at George Washington University has the courage to become emotionally involved with her patients. She advocates for spirituality in the treatment of illness and disease. She does not shy away from the hardest and sickest patients. She says she and the patient have both been enriched by her being a "compassionate presence" and friend to her patients. She says that even terminal patients must always have hope: hope for a cure, hope for healing, hope for finishing important goals, hope for a peaceful death. . She says that every patient can be healed, although not necessarily restored to physical health. Healing is the restoration of "wholeness" We all can and should become whole- especially before we die and return to our Heavenly Father. Hope is an integral part of wholeness and something we can all achieve even in the most difficult circumstances.

I would like to give you an example of a dear friend of mine who is a good example of the virtues I have been extolling in this chapter. Chris Miller was a fellow employee and social worker who always had a smile on his face and had a quick wit. He could always make me laugh and he had a great sense of humor. He was also known for his compassion. As social workers, we are sometimes required to be "on-call" and this would require helping transients. We would typically get the transient a bus ticket or some gas to help them on their way. Chris, however, would go way beyond what was expected. He would get his person a hot meal and go through his own closet to give them a coat or some much needed clothing. During the prime of his life, he was diagnosed with cancer. He had four children at home including an infant. Chris, however, did not complain but accepted his illness with faith.

No matter how hard he fought, the disease only worsened. Chris's optimism did not fade even though the disease finally took his life. The veil became thin prior to his death and he could be heard talking to deceased family members that were invisible to the rest of us. I visited with Chris a few days prior to his death. He said he was tired but otherwise he felt fine. He seemed to be at peace. At times I felt Chris was too good for this earth life and was called home by his Heavenly Father. He is a wonderful example of a person who never lost hope despite his dire circumstances. He went through tremendous suffering but he did not become depressed. He passed away peacefully and sweetly.

We can promote this hope by keeping God's commandments, praying, reading scripture and be-lieving Christ. As Ether said this hope can become an "anchor to our soul" Also we need to foster an attitude that is open to learning no matter what the circumstance.

CHAPTER 15

In conclusion

Many of these things that I have discussed in this book hit close to home. I have experienced some of the problems in this book. I speak to you not only as a therapist but as a former sufferer who is completely recovered. I suffered from depression many years ago but recovered. It was a horrific experience I do not wish to repeat. I do not believe that I will repeat that experience again because I have acquired all the skills and tools I need to ward off depression. Also some of my old core beliefs have changed and I have acquired new, healthier core beliefs. But the depression I experienced was a tremendous learning experience for me. I am a stronger, better person because of it. It has given me some insight into my clients' suffering that I do not believe classes and study could have produced. In the grand councils of heavens before I was born, I probably agreed with the Lord that I needed to go through that experience for my benefit and learning so I could in turn help others.

There is no one who waltzes effortlessly through life. As I stated earlier, I do not believe that the Lord intends for any of us to have to spend a lifetime suffering. However, we will all be called to go through our own personal Gethsemanes. This could be in the form of a mental or emotional disorder, such as depression, anxiety disorder, eating disorder, bi-polar disorder or even schizophrenia. Or it could come in the form of some physical disorder or illness, such as cancer or multiple sclerosis. As is often the case, a person could be living a very happy, carefree life when he is hit with tragedy, such as an accident or the death of a loved one. Or a person may have to suffer at the hands of another as in the case of assault or sexual abuse. Just when we seem to be batting a thousand then life throws us a curve. However, through it all, Heavenly Father expects us to endure the trial patiently and somehow over come it. Even in the case of a terminal illness that eventually takes our life, we must somehow rise above the fear and bitterness and achieve hope and peace.

One of my favorite scriptures is appropriate here. In Ether, Moroni interjects some of his own comments. He is lamenting to the Lord about his and the Nephites' weakness for writing. He is afraid that when the *Book of Mormon* record comes forth in the latter days, the Gentiles will scoff. However, the Lord reassures him and says this inspiring statement:

"And if men come unto me I will show them their weakness. I give unto men weakness that they may be humble; and my grace is sufficient for all men that humble themselves before me; for if they humble themselves before me, and have faith in me, then will I make weak thing become strong unto them" (Ether 12:23)

During these crisis periods when the Lord reveals our weaknesses to us we can be permanently weakened, disabled or destroyed. On the other hand, we can also be ultimately strengthened and eventually achieve greater happiness and joy. There are three essential steps we must take during these crisis periods that will help us to endure well and, in the end, be strengthened by the Lord.

First, as I have emphasized throughout this book, we must think as clearly and rationally as we possibly can. Our negative thoughts are like the strong wind that can turn a small brush fire into a raging fire that burns down the whole forest. Our thoughts can turn a bad situation into something much worse. We all think the worst sometimes but we must constantly rein in those negative thoughts and replace them with positive, realistic and logical thoughts. We must take the time to "collect ourselves" when hard times come and look at the situation from many different angles and decide on the best course of action. Do not trust the initial negative thoughts because they tend to be distorted and not based on reality. As the Lord stated in Isaiah, "Come, let us reason together" and think through the problem logically and rationally.

The second step in enduring trials and challenges is the importance of asking for help. Contrary to what many people may think, asking for help is not a sign of weakness but a sign of strength. We need to be selective about who we talk to but a wise person will always seek for counsel when he is feeling overwhelmed, discouraged or worried. He may choose to talk to a trusted friend, family member, priesthood leader, therapist or doctor. These people can often help us to think through our problems objectively and give us much needed guidance and direction. Plus, just the act of talking is therapeutic and helps us to feel better.

Finally, rely upon God and the Holy Ghost during times of trial. Spend much time in prayer, scripture study and fasting. It is a very humbling and sometimes a painful process but we must go through that "searching and fearless moral inventory" spoken of in the twelve steps. We must examine ourselves with a critical eye before the Lord and lay out our weaknesses and problems plainly before Him. This does not mean that we utterly degrade ourselves and think of ourselves as worthless. But we must take full responsibility for our weaknesses and humbly ask for help. The help will come in different ways. Perhaps it will come in the form of an impression or prompting while we are praying or meditating Perhaps it will come in the form of a caring bishop, parent, friend or counselor. We must never give up hope that the help and direction will come. We must have faith that we will somehow overcome this trial with the Lord's help. These three steps have greatly helped me in my life and I trust it will also benefit you.

Once a person has eliminated the self defeating behaviors in his life and his weaknesses have been converted into strengths; once a person has corrected his thinking and has developed healthy core beliefs; and finally, once a person has managed to have the Spirit in his life on a daily basis then that person becomes mentally healthy and achieves that elusive quality called happiness. Even though we will be tested and have periods of discouragement and stress, the Lord intends for his children to be happy. As stated in the scriptures: "men are that they might have joy" (2 Nephi 2:25) I remember quoting this scripture to one poor woman who had suffered from depression for many years. She looked at me and with all sincerity asked "Do you think that means we can be happy in this life time?" I assured her that this scripture applies to this lifetime and God wants his children to be happy in this lifetime. One can see people who have achieved happiness in this lifetime. They have found that pot of gold at the end of the rainbow. As I think about our dear prophet, Gordon B. Hinckley, he exemplifies one who has captured happiness in his life. Individuals such as him seem to have a perennial smile on their faces and they positively radiate. They are excited and enthused about life. There seems to be nothing that will stop them. They have experienced trials in their lives, but they have success-fully overcome them. This is the way it will be in heaven but even more so. Those of us who make it to the highest degree of heaven will be in a constant state of joy and happiness. Isn't it wonderful that we can also experience heaven on earth? This is my prayer for every one that we all can catch heaven on earth and experience joy.

REFERENCES

Introduction
1. Journal of Consulting and Clinical Psychology 1980 Vol. 48.

2. Matthews, D. A. Faith Factor NY: Viking Press, 1998, pp. 60-83.

3. Ibid. p. 25.

4. Ibid. p. 85.

Chapter 2
1. Ellis, A. & Harper, R.A. A New Guide to Rational Living England, CA: Prentice Hall, 1961.

Chapter 5
1. Hafen, B. Broken Heart S.L.C.: Deseret Book, 1989 ppg. 137, 139.

2. Beck, A., Rush, A.J., Shaw, B.F., Emery, G. Cognitive Therapy of Depression NY: Guilford Press, 1979. pp. 164-165.

Chapter 6
1. Peck, M.S. Road Less Traveled NY: Touchstone Book, 1978. p. 35.

2. Scott. R. "To Help a Loved One in Need" Ensign, May, 1988. p. 50.

3. Hidden Treasures Institute. Hold On To Hope CFI: Springville, UT 1996. pp. 97-98.

4. Beck. A. Rush, A.J. p. 159.

5. Greenburger, D. & Padesky, C.A. Mind Over Mood NY: Guilford Press, 1995 ppg. 201-207.
6. Hidden Treasures Institute. p. 99.

Chapter 7
1. Bergin, S. <u>BYU Today</u> Provo: Brigham Young University Press. March, 1989. p 39.

2. Young, B. <u>Journal of Discourses</u> 11:132.

3. Newsweek "We Can Handle It" Dec. 3, 2001. p 30-33.

4. Gardner, M.K. "Elder Russell M. Nelson: Applying Divine Laws" <u>Ensign</u> June, 1984 p. 9.

5. Holland, J & Holland, P <u>On Earth As It Is In Heaven</u> S.L: Deseret Book, 1989 p. 65.

6. Benson, H. <u>Relaxation Response</u> NY: Avon Books, 1975.

Chapter 8
1. Meichenbaum, D. 7th Counseling Skills Conference "Emerging Issues in Counseling" Oct. 2-4, 2001.

2. Deseret News "Heaps of Diamonds Help Fund War in the Congo." May 20, 2001. p. A13.

3. Sports Illustrated. "Miracle on the Mat. American Gardner Stuns Karelin in huge upset." Sep. 27, 2000.

4. Ibid. p 47.

5. Greenburger, D. & Padesky, C.A. pp. 143-144.

6. Excerpt from Nelson's Mandela's 1994 Inaugural Speech.

Chapter 9
1. Weekes, C. <u>Hope and Help for Your Nerves</u> Toronto: Bantam Books, 1969
2, Ford, D. <u>Secret of the Shadow</u> Harper: San Francisco, 2002 p. 64 & 66.

3. Hallowell, N. 7th counseling Skills Conference "Emerging

Issues In Counseling" Las Vegas. Oct. 4-6, 2001.

Chapter 10
1. LDS Speakers Source Book S.L.C.: Aspen Books, 1991 p.
57, 189; Teachings of Gordon B. Hinckley S.L.C.: Deseret
Book, 1997 p 25-26.

2. Ubell, E. "The Deadly Emotions" Parade Magazine
February 11, 1990 pp 4-6.

3. Teachings of the Presidents of the Church: Brigham Young
Church of Jesus Christ of Latter Day Saints, 1995 pp. 205-
206.

4. Covey, S. The 7 Habits of Highly Effective People N.Y:
Simon & Shuster, 1989 p 204.

Chapter 11
1. Chamberlain, J.M.   Eliminate Your SDBs Provo: Brigham
Young University Press, 1978.

2. Epstein, R. "Change Your Bad Habits to Good" Readers
Digest October, 1998 pp 25-30.

3. Beattie, M. Co-dependent No More S.F: Harper & Row,
1989.

4. Hidden Treasures Institute, chapters 7,8, 9.

Chapter 12
1. Lowery, C & Lowery, M.   The Fourth Annual Summer
Institute, Graduate School of Social Work, University of Utah.
July, 1988. "Coping With Depression: State of the Art of
Diagnosis and Treatment."

2. Diagnostic and Statistical Manual IV American Psychiatric
Association, 1994 p. 684.

3. Lundberg, K The Fourteenth Annual Summer Institute,
Graduate School of Social Work, University of Utah, July,

1998 "Grief."

Chapter 13
1. Beck. A, Rush, R.A., p. 164.

2. Smith, L. N. Spirituality & Healing in Medicine conference "The Principles of Spiritual Well Being: Methods for Applying These Principles in Clinical Practice" Salt Lake City March, 2002.

3. Benson, H. Beyond the Relaxation Response NY: Berkley Books, 1984.

4. Top, B.L. & Chadwick, B.A. "Raising Righteous Children in a Wicked World" BYU Today Summer, 1998, pp. 41-51.

5. Peeke, P. Fight Fat after Forty NY: Viking Press, 2000, chapter 4.

6. Covey. S. Habit 7: pp. 287-309.

Chapter 14
1. Frankl, F.E. Man's Search for Meaning N.Y: Touchstone Book, 1984. p.148.

2. Ibid.

3. Pulchaski, C.M. "Spiritual Care in a Clinical Setting" Spirituality & Healing in Medicine conference. Salt Lake City, March 14-16, 2002.

Like many people, I grew up in a dysfunctional family. Ours had an alcoholic father. My response to that environment was an attraction to addictive personalities with me in the role of enabler. For years I sought to change this behavior through faith without combining it with clinical practice. This faith-alone approach was sometimes helpful, but familiar behavior patterns continued to occur. When I read *Spiritual Therapy*, a light, a ray of hope entered my life. I could feel that combining professional ideas with spiritual concepts bridges the void between the two. Also, I found the book very readable and enjoyable. I refer to it often for guidance in my quest to heal. I value this book so much that I introduced it to my bishop and stake presidency with the hope that they will use it to assist in people-problems they encounter. *Spiritual Therapy* is a book that can change lives.

Bonita Robertson, MS, RN
Head of Nursing (retired)
Salt Lake Comm. College

Jim Shelton offers amazingly simple and effective solutions to complex dilemmas and problems that everyone faces. The pages of *Spiritual Therapy* shine with his warmth, humility, wisdom and experience. This book is mandatory reading for anyone seeking to build, heal, and improve his life!

Cliff R. Passey, M.Ed., MSW
LDS Seminary Teacher

If hope is a vision of God's promises and the road that leads to them, then Jim Shelton has written a very hopeful book. He himself has walked the road leading out of depression, and that in itself is a message of hope. The cognitive therapy he espouses can silence the internal voices that tear at our hope of healing and wholeness, allowing the Savior's voice to speak peace and promise. I recommend this book, *Spiritual Therapy*, to anyone seeking these blessings.

Larry Lewis, L.P.C.
Clinical Supervisor
LDS Family Services

More reading from Archive Publishers:

Answers to Questions (George A. Smith)	6.95
Are We of Israel? (George Reynolds)	6.95
Blood Atonement & Plural Marriage (Joseph Fielding Smith)	7.95
Book of Commandments (1833 Edition)	9.95
Book of John Whitmer, The (John Whitmer)	9.95
Book of Mormon, The (1830 Edition)	23.95
Brief History of the Church, A (Edward H. Anderson)	12.95
Catechism for Children (John Jacques)	6.95
Collection of Deseret's Pioneer Stories, A	8.95
Collection of Facts about Sidney Rigdon (Jedediah M. Grant)	7.95
Concise History of the Mormon Battalion, A (Daniel Tyler)	20.95
Diet Decisions for Latter-day Saints (Joyce Kinmont)	12.95
Does the Bible Sanction Polygamy (Orson Pratt)	12.95
Edmunds Law & Unlawful Cohabitation Defined, The	9.95
Elders of Israel and the Constitution (Jerome Horowitz)	13.95
Elders of Israel Study Guide (Jerome Horowitz)	16.95
For Our Little Friends (Deseret Sunday School)	9.95
Founding of Utah, The Vol. 1&2 (Levi Edgar Young)	21.95
From Kirtland to Salt Lake City (James A. Little)	15.95
From Plowboy to Prophet (William A. Morton)	9.95
Good Stories for Boys & Girls (William A. Morton)	11.95
Gospel, The (B. H. Roberts)	17.95
Government of God, The (John Taylor)	9.95
Great and Abominable Church of the Devil (H. Verlan Andersen)	14.95
Great Apostasy, The (James E. Talmage)	12.95
Greatest Sermons & Writings of Latter-day Prophets	12.95
History of Joseph Smith for Youth, The (George Q. Cannon)	13.95
House of the Lord, The (James E. Talmage)	19.95
John Taylor: Educator (Jack Monnett)	7.95
Joseph Smith as Scientist (John A. Widtsoe)	12.95
Joseph Smith Monument Dedication	11.95
Joseph Smith: the Prophet/Teacher (B. H. Roberts)	6.95
Joseph Smith, Prophet—1853 Edition (Lucy Mack Smith)	15.95
Joseph Smith's Views on Power & Policy of Government	5.95
Key to Succession in Presidency (P. J. Sanders)	14.95
Key to the Science of Theology (Parley P. Pratt)	12.95
Key to the Universe (Orson Pratt)	9.95
LDS Emigrants' Guide (William Clayton)	4.95
Lectures on Faith (1835 Edition)	6.95
Legal Basis of a Free Society, The (H. Verlan Andersen)	14.95
Life and Labors of Eliza R. Snow (Funeral Remarks)	5.95

Life of Brigham Young, The (Edward H. Anderson)	12.95
Life of David Patten, The (Lycurgus A. Wilson)	7.95
Life of Orson Spencer & History of Primary (Aurelia Rogers)	19.95
Many Are Called, But Few Are Chosen (H. Verlan Andersen)	7.95
Martyrdom of Joseph Smith & The Mormons (Taylor/Kane)	8.95
Martyrdom of Joseph Standing, The (John Nicholson)	11.95
Martyrs, The (Lyman O. Littlefield)	9.95
Mediation & Atonement of Jesus Christ, The (John Taylor)	13.95
Memoirs of John R. Young, The (John R. Young)	20.95
Missouri Persecutions, The (B. H. Roberts)	19.95
Mormon Battalion, The (B. H. Roberts)	9.95
Mormon Prophet's Tragedy, The (Orson F. Whitney)	8.95
Mormon Settlement in Arizona (James H. McClintock)	19.95
Mother Stories from the Book of Mormon (William A. Morton)	10.95
My Life's Review (Benjamin F. Johnson)	21.95
Origin of the "Reorganized" Church (Joseph Fielding Smith)	9.95
Outlines of Ecclesiastical History (B. H. Roberts)	22.95
Parley P. Pratt Reader, A (Parley P. Pratt)	9.95
Proper Role of Government (Ezra Taft Benson/H. Verlan Andersen)	5.95
Prophecies of Joseph Smith & Fulfillment (Nephi Morris)	13.95
Relationship of Mormonism to Freemasonry (A. W. Ivins)	13.95
Revealed Ed. Principles & Public Schools (Jack Monnett)	15.95
Rise & Fall of Nauvoo, The (B. H. Roberts)	22.95
Spiritual Therapy (Jim Shelton)	11.95
Successful Missionary, The (John A. Widtsoe)	7.95
Tennessee Massacre & Utah Conspiracy (John Nicholson)	7.95
Thrilling Experiences (Solomon F. Kimball)	9.95
United States Has Two Constitutions, The (Jerome Horowitz)	14.95
View of the Hebrews (Ethan Smith)	14.95
Voice of Warning, A (Parley P. Pratt)	12.95
White Indian Boy / Among the Shoshones (Elijah N. Wilson)	14.95
Young Folks History of the LDS Church, A (Nephi Anderson)	12.95

Archive Publishers
754 East 50 North
Heber City, UT 84032

www.archivepublishers.com
email:info@archivepublishers.com
(435) 654-0824   Fax: (435) 654-4289

February 1, 2010

More reading from Archive Publishers:

NON-LDS BOOKS

Abraham Lincoln (Wilbur F. Gordy)	15.95
Alfred the Great (Jacob Abbott)	13.95
America's Founding Documents	5.95
Apocryphal New Testament, The	16.95
Bach: The Boy from Thuringia (Opal Wheeler & Sybil Deucher)	9.95
Book of Enoch, The	12.95
Book of Jasher, The	15.95
Children of History, The (Mary S. Hancock)	13.95
Franklin: The Apprentice Boy (Jacob Abbott)	11.95
Inspiration a Day, An (Rhanda Hunter Todd)	17.95
Island Story, An Vol. 1&2 (H.E. Marshall)	24.95
Mother of Washington (Nancy Turner & Sidney Gunn)	16.95
Nursery, The Vol. 1	12.95
Nursery, The Vol. 2	12.95
Our Home, Vol. 1&2 (C.E. Sargent)	21.95
Play It Book, Days of Games for Children, The (Jean Fretwell)	10.95
Stories of American Explorers and Settlers (Heard & King)	15.95
Story Hour, The (Kate Douglas Wiggin & Nora A. Smith)	12.95
This Blessed Land (Lezlee Jones)	15.95
War of Independence, The (John Fiske)	13.95

Archive Publishers
754 East 50 North
Heber City, UT 84032

www.archivepublishers.com
email: info@archivepublishers.com
(435) 654-0824   Fax: (435) 654-4289

January 1, 2010